Tips for Teaching ESL/EFL to Teenagers, University Students & Adults: A Practical Guide

Jackie Bolen

(www.eslspeaking.org)

Table of Contents

About the Author: Jackie Bolen...6
    Jackie Bolen around the Internet...6
How to Use this Book...7
General English Teaching Tips...8
    Consider Teaching some Classroom English..8
    Avoid Putting People on the Spot (Usually)..9
    Reasons to Avoid Microphones...9
    Tips for Giving Instructions..10
    Tips for Monitoring Activities...11
    Top 10 Tips for Making English Classes Interesting..11
    Give Students a Choice Whenever Possible..12
    Tips for Teaching Multi-Level Classes..13
    Be in Class Before the Students Arrive Whenever Possible.............................14
    Consider NOT Grading Participation...14
    Don't Forget your CCQ's (Check for Understanding)..16
Classroom Behavior Management Strategies...18
    Keep Emotions in Check...18
    Private Scolding is Better than Public...18
    Practice Positive Reinforcement...19
    Recognize Teacher Caused Behavioural Issues and Stop Them.....................19
    Avoid Dead-Time..22
    Don't Forget about Eye Contact and Pay Attention to Dead Spots..................22
    Tips for Gaining Respect of the Students after You've Lost It..........................22
    Tips for Helping Students who are Reluctant to Participate in Class..............24
Tips for Lesson Planning...26
    Assess the Level of your Students...26
    Fail to Plan = Plan to Fail..27
    Use at Least a Basic Lesson Plan..28
    Recycle Teaching Materials Whenever Possible..29
    Be Realistic about How Much Material Can be Covered..................................29
    Let Students Know Where they're Going..30
    Tips for Giving Homework..30
    Stop the Homework Madness, Part 1..31
    Stop the Homework Madness, Part 2..31
    Tips for What to Do After a Terrible Lesson...33
    Tips for Dealing with Terrible Textbooks..34
    Consider Using Warm-Ups..34
    Lone Ranger all the Way for Lesson Planning!..35
    Use Level Appropriate Language..36
    Tips for Beginning a Class...37
Tips for Teaching English to Teenage or Adult Beginners.......................................39
    Teach a Few Things, a Lot...39
    It's All About Review..39
    Consider Topics Carefully..39
    Avoid Surprises in the ESL Classroom...40

Ask Students if they Want Homework...41
Ask for Feedback and Be Willing to Adapt..41
Offer Lots of Encouragement and Praise..42
Remember that Students are Good at Other Things..42
All About Teaching Writing to ESL Beginners..43
Tips for Avoiding the English Teacher Burnout Thing..46
Look after Yourself...46
Just Use the Textbook!..46
For Tests, Simple is Best!..47
Learn to Say No...48
Consider Overtime Carefully..48
Motivation isn't Just for the Students...48
Think about Work Space...49
Stay on Top of the Paperwork...50
Keep Moving Onwards and Upwards...50
Think about Life After Teaching..51
Tips for Teaching Speaking...52
Listening is Important Too..52
Lessons Don't Always Need to be Fun...52
Change Partners Often..53
Give Feedback...53
Use the Whiteboard for Key Words and Phrases..54
Change Up Activities Frequently..55
Repetition is Key...55
Keep Fluency + Accuracy in Balance...56
Tips for Teaching Low Level Speaking Classes...57
Consider Doing Some Presentations in Speaking or Conversation Classes.................60
Tips for Making a More Student-Centered Classroom...61
Consider Using this Speaking Rubric for Tests..63
Tips for Teaching Listening...67
Students have Different Needs in Terms of Listening..67
Figure out the Technology Before Class Starts 67
How Many Times Should I Play the Listening Passage?...68
Consider Some Listening Focused Lessons in Conversation Classes..........................68
Listening Passages: Check the Textbook First...69
Listening Exercises: Ideal for Homework Assignments...69
Listen for One Specific Thing...69
It's Not Just about Native Speakers from North America...70
Give Students a Reason to Listen..70
Don't Forget About Two-Way Communication!..71
Get Familiar with Listening Sub-Skills..71
Use this ESL Listening Lesson Plan Template...74
Tips for Finding Listening Passages...76
Tips for Teaching Writing..80
Student-Centred Teaching is ALWAYS Best...80
Use a Grading Rubric for Evaluating Writing..81
Giving Feedback when Teaching Writing..84

Which ESL Writing Textbook Do you Recommend?...85
  How Do I Prevent Cheating in a Writing Class?...86
  How Can I Foster Student Autonomy in Writing Classes?...................................87
  Include Writing in Speaking and Conversation Classes.......................................89
  Teach the Writing Process...90
  All About Writing Style..90
  Read Good Quality Models of the Target Writing Style......................................91
  Mistakes are Unavoidable..92
  Don't Forget about Writing Fluency Practice...93
  What Can Students Write About? 95
Tips for Teaching Grammar..100
  Avoid Rocking the Chalk..100
  Music and Videos: Ideal for Teaching English Grammar...................................101
  Use Short Stories or Cartoons..102
  Don't Forget About Context..104
  Grammar Requires Other Skills to Teach It..104
  Brush up on the Grammar Yourself...105
  Keep It Simple...105
  Use this English Grammar Lesson Plan Template...106
Tips for Teaching Reading..109
  It's Not Just About Reading for Detail...109
  Consider Students' Needs..112
  Vocabulary is Important...113
  Use a Variety of Comprehension Questions..114
  Does it Apply to Real-Life?...114
  Sneak in Some Pronunciation...114
  Use Authentic Materials for Higher-Level Students..116
  Teach Reading Strategies...116
  Use this 7 Step ESL Reading Lesson Plan...117
Before You Go...121

Copyright © 2020 by Jackie Bolen

All rights reserved. No part of this publication may be reproduced, distributed, or transmitted in any form or by any means, including photocopying, recording or other electronic or mechanical means without the prior written permission of the publisher, except in the case of brief quotations in critical reviews and certain other non-commercial uses permitted by copyright law. For permission requests, write to the publisher/author at the address below.

Jackie Bolen: jb.business.online@gmail.com

About the Author: Jackie Bolen

I taught English in South Korea for a decade to every level and type of student. I've taught every age from kindergarten kids to adults. Most of my time centered around teaching at two universities: five years at a science and engineering school out in the rice paddies of Chungcheongnam-Do, and four years at a major university in Busan where I taught high level classes for students majoring in English. I now teach ESL/EFL students in Vancouver, Canada. In my spare time, you can usually find me outside surfing, biking, hiking, or on the hunt for the most delicious kimchi I can find. It's not so easy in Vancouver!

In case you were wondering what my academic qualifications are, I hold a Master of Arts Degree in Psychology. During my time in Korea I successfully completed both the Cambridge CELTA and DELTA certification programs. With the combination of fifteen years teaching ESL/EFL learners of all ages and levels, and the more formal teaching qualifications I obtained, I have a solid foundation on which to offer teaching advice. I truly hope that you find this book useful and would love it if you sent me an email with any questions or feedback that you might have.

Jackie Bolen around the Internet

ESL Speaking (www.eslactivity.org)

Jackie Bolen (www.jackiebolen.com)

Twitter: @bolen_jackie

Email: jb.business.online@gmail.com

You may also want to check out some of other books on *Amazon* (search for Jackie Bolen), but here are a few of my most popular titles:

39 No-Prep/Low-Prep ESL Speaking Activities

39 Awesome 1-1 ESL Activities

101 ESL Activities for Teenagers and Adults

Life After ESL: Foreign Teachers Returning Home

How to Use this Book

If you want to have better ESL/EFL classes, then reading this book is a helpful step along that path. It has a wealth of very practical tips from a teacher who has experience in a number of different teaching situations. Newbies will find it immensely valuable. However, even veteran teachers can pick up some tips and inspiration.

As for how to use the book, you could certainly consider reading it from cover to cover. Another idea is to quickly scan the table of contents for the situation most pertinent to you. For example, teaching writing can be quite a different experience than speaking. However, all teachers will benefit from the section on general teaching tips, avoiding burnout, as well as lesson planning.

I hope that this book is useful to you! Please feel free to get in touch with me via email (jb.business.online@gmail.com) or *Facebook* (www.facebook.com/eslspeaking) if you have any questions that I might be able to assist you with. Good luck and here's to better English teaching!

General English Teaching Tips

Consider Teaching some Classroom English

There are phrases that your students will need to know and understand, so you should be prepared to devote some class time in the beginning, if your students are low level. Even if they are not beginners, they may not recall the vocabulary, or they may be accustomed to being given instructions in their first language.

With my lower level students, I try to keep instructions short and to the point, but I still add please and thank you. It gets them in the habit of mentally tacking it on to a request, but shouldn't overwhelm them with the volume of language being thrown at them.

If your students are really low level, consider having posters/anchor charts around your room with useful phrases and an associated image to remind them of the meaning. Some of these are:

1. Sit down, please. Stand up, please.
2. Take out/Put away _____, please.
3. Turn to page/exercise _____, please.
4. Repeat, please.
5. In English, please.
6. With a partner/In groups of _____, please.
7. Louder/Quieter, please.
8. Look/Listen/Look and listen, please.
9. Your turn.
10. All together/One at a time, please.
11. Let's begin.

Obviously, this is not an exhaustive list, but throw in some numbers and school supplies, and you would be surprised how many of your instructions boil down to these phrases.

Please/Thank You/May I/Sorry

Non-native speakers have a bit of an excuse, but there's no time like the present to learn basic manners. When I practice asking, giving, and receiving with language, I emphasize that these words are for everyone, not just when speaking to adults. I model, "May I borrow _____, please?"

"Here you are."

"Thank you."

"You're welcome."

Then, I have students practice with their neighbour. Even though I try to keep the number of words I speak low, I add please, thank you, and you're welcome to all requests. Even beginner students can understand, "Page 10, please," just as well as, "Page 10."

Avoid Putting People on the Spot (Usually)

This is a big no-no in Korea and in many other parts of Asia too. No ones like to feel shame because they didn't know the answer. To avoid this, I'll always give the students some pre-practice before I elicit an answer, either by doing some writing in their books, or speaking with their partner or in a small group. Of course, comparing answers with a partner before doing it in front of the whole class is a great strategy to use.

If I am going to choose a student or two to share their answer with the entire class, I'll usually give them a heads up during this compare with a partner time so that they know it's coming and can get ready for it.

Reasons to Avoid Microphones

Whenever I go into classrooms that only have 20 or 30 desks filling up the entire space, there is always a microphone that has been put to obvious use in the immediate class before me. Like it's actually sitting on the podium, turned on and I always wonder why.

Who actually has such a small voice that they can't project it enough for a class of 20 or 30 people? Does anyone actually just stand at the podium and lecture the entire time? Does anyone actually like holding a microphone in their hand for 75 minutes?

Most importantly, do students actually LIKE listening to a voice that is microphone projected, with a low-quality sound system and crappy microphone? I occasionally make use of the speakers for a few minutes to watch a short video or do a little listening thing and they annoy me during that short time, such that I even refuse to use them for more than a few minutes each class.

Think about Error Correction

You may want to make note of some correct and incorrect uses of the target language you heard being practiced during an activity or game. Without naming names, write a few good examples and offer some praise for creative use of language, or whatever.

Then, write a few mistakes and show how to correct them. For example, "I heard some students saying, "I don't like the apples, but it would be better to say, I don't like apples. Do you know why?"

Tips for Giving Instructions

KISS applies in spades here. Keep It Simple, Stupid (or Sweetie, if that's how you roll.) Using extra words will crowd the important ones and overwhelm your students. Reduce your instructions to the minimum number of words necessary for them to carry out a task correctly. I don't mean use baby talk; I just mean don't give them a stream of consciousness rambling monologue or 300 words when 30 will suffice. Enunciate clearly, and pause between chunks of information to let your students process what you have said.

Additionally, the lower your students' level the more you will need to adjust your language. For higher level students, you want to speak fairly naturally, but without too much slang or informal language. For beginners, you will want to slow down, repeat key words or phrases, pause often, use gestures and miming (when appropriate), and stick to vocabulary they know. If a set of instructions is met with a sea of blank faces, don't be afraid to back it up and say it again, differently and/or more slowly and clearly.

Some other strategies for making sure that students understand instructions are to write down the key steps on the board or PowerPoint, highlighting the main action words. Also consider doing a quick demonstration of the activity.

Tips for Monitoring Activities

While your students are working, you should be moving around the class, watching and listening. If you are at your desk or the front of the class, you may not be aware of students who need help. Few students like to call attention to the fact that they need help. Often students will look busy and engaged from a distance, but will either be off-task or trying to follow instructions they misunderstood.

As you walk around, you will see who needs help. You will also get an idea of what kinds of questions students have but may not want to ask. You can avoid singling anyone out, by addressing the class, "I saw a number or people talking in big groups, but remember that it's actually a 1-1 speaking activity." If a number of students seem to be making the same mistakes, then you can back things up and provide more examples or guided practice.

Another benefit of moving through the classroom while students work, is that students are less likely to goof off if they know you are more likely to catch them. A student in the back of the class has little difficulty looking engaged from the white board. A conversation and a practice dialogue look pretty similar, if you can't hear them and aren't watching closely.

Top 10 Tips for Making English Classes Interesting

There are a number of things you can do to make your English lessons more interesting. Here are my top ten ideas:

- Use student-centered activities so that they are more engaged with the lesson

objective/s and language practice/learning
- Use a wide variety of games and activities
- Use technology, but not all the time
- Laugh and have fun with the students
- Think about interactive lessons above all else
- Consider task-based activities
- Change groups and partners often
- Get outside (make sure that this is not against admin policy) if the weather is nice by doing something like a picture quest or scavenger hunt
- Think about how to get students out of their seats and moving around the class.

Give Students a Choice Whenever Possible

Most people like a say in what they do and your students are no different. As often as possible, offer a choice to your students. Of course, you may need to limit the choices, but it gives them a bit of control of their learning.

There are a few ways to do this. One is to simply offer a few options for the production phase of the lesson. For example, "Your team can either make a poster about _____ to present to the class, or each team member can add one, four sentence paragraph to a group essay on the same topic." Another way to offer choices is with homework.

I have a variety of early finisher tasks so there is something for everyone. Students who like to read can always read a book. Others can practice grammar or vocabulary with task cards. Students who prefer drawing to English can draw a picture and write about it. You may have to watch that last one, though. Plenty of students manage to time the drawing portion of the activity to fill the entire gap. You can always present it to them the next time they finish early, of course.

Tips for Teaching Multi-Level Classes

This challenge requires a lot of planning and still will probably not be perfect. When there are students who barely know the alphabet studying alongside near-fluent students who've studied in an English speaking country, it can be a difficult task. There are two basic ways to deal with it and I like to use both at different times.

The first is to create levelled groups, so that higher-level students work together and lower-level students work together. You can give each group a level-appropriate assignment based on what you are studying. For example, if your textbook has you teaching like/don't like, have your lower level students use a stack of flashcards and take turns asking and answering questions with a partner, based on the flashcard they draw. Your highest level students can create a dialogue about why they like or don't like a TV show, book, computer game, or whatever. If they are really high level, have them add a persuasive element. In-between groups should be given tasks that are between the two in difficulty.

One thing to consider about this approach is that it can be difficult to monitor and give feedback to students who are all doing different things. If you opt for this route, it's much easier to pull off in a class with fewer than 12 students. For bigger classes, it's still possible if you have a co-teacher who can also offer feedback and error correction assistance.

The second approach is to have mixed level groups or pairs and have the higher level student(s) tutor the lower level one(s). Both students benefit from this arrangement and you don't have to be everywhere at once.

You probably noticed the common theme is small group and pair work. If you try to have everyone work as individuals, you can really only teach to the middle. At best, you'll be left with two groups of students zoned out (the strongest and the weakest ones) who are equally likely to start causing trouble out of boredom. In any case, pair and group work are a natural fit for ESL, because they require students to communicate, and isn't that what you want?

If you can't segregate students in this way, or if you have too many classes which you see too infrequently to know each student's level, you can give everyone the same set of tasks, but have the tasks become increasingly difficult. The higher level students will be challenged by the work at the end. The lower level students will be working at a slower pace, so will still be challenged, but hopefully not overwhelmed.

To be honest, I put this last, because it is the most work and also my least-favorite option. The lower level students will see that they are never finishing the work you set out for them and who wants to be reassured by being told they were never expected to be capable of finishing? Not me. But, some type of differentiation is still better than teaching to the middle, in my opinion.

Be in Class Before the Students Arrive Whenever Possible

Nothing looks less professional than someone who rushes around after the students are already in the class, struggling to get the PPT fired up and all their papers out.

Contrast this to someone who is prepared by the time most of the students are there and is able to personally greet each one as they walk in the door, in a relaxed, Zen-like kind of way. I personally prefer this whenever possible, if only for my own mental health.

Consider NOT Grading Participation

I personally don't like grading participation in my classes and will only do it if absolutely required by the administration. Mostly, I just find it to be a huge hassle and not worth the effort. Here are a few reasons why I don't grade participation.

Mastery of Course Content

Isn't mastering the course content important, more so than effort at a certain level, especially for university students? At some point (perhaps high-school?), it's time to just expect competence in something especially if the students have been studying it for years.

If a student has been studying English for eight years but doesn't have a grasp on simple past questions or negatives, perhaps it's time for them to figure it out in my class!

Participation Reflected in the Final Grade

Good students will participate in class, but will also do the best on tests and homework. In my experience, removing participation grades actually has no effect whatsoever on final grades. It's just way more work for the teacher for basically no change in the actual grades of the students.

What about Introverted Students?

Grading participation in language classes really, really favours extroverted students. As kind of an introvert myself, I have a lot of sympathy for these kinds of people and I really do think it's unfair that quiet people get punished. Just because someone is quiet, it doesn't mean that they're not participating in your class. They certainly could be listening far more intently and following instructions better than the loud extrovert.

Why do the Task?

You are failing as a teacher if you ever get into the situation where students are only doing a task because they'll get some participation points. There are plenty of far better reasons for students to do tasks than this.

What Criteria to Use for Grading?

Grading participation all seems so subjective and biased and I would argue that it basically comes down to giving points to the students that you like and taking away points from the students that you don't. This certainly isn't my style and I try to never, ever play favourites. Even if you try not to do this, it's pretty hard to avoid when you're handing out participation points.

The other thing to consider is that if someone ever questions your grading, it's so easy to point to a test or piece of homework to justify yourself. Participation points? How could you ever justify this? Min-Su spoke 17 times, but Ji-Su only spoke 11 times. Min-Ji looked happy but Ji-Won was always grumpy. It's not ideal, right?

What's your Job?

I personally would rather be a facilitator of learning than a full-time assessor. I like to help out to the best of my ability while in class and judge only on tests. Finally, I hope that my students can just relax and enjoy the class and not feel like I'm always watching them. Big Brother just ain't my style, you know?

Students Don't Care About It

When I asked my students, most of them don't seem to care one way or the other whether I grade participation in class. It's a lot of work and so if students don't care about it, it doesn't really make sense to use this criteria in grading.

Don't Forget your CCQ's (Check for Understanding)

When I did the CELTA course, it was ALL about CCQ's. It stands for concept checking question. Basically, when you teach something to the students, for example, a new vocabulary or grammatical concept, don't finish with, "Okay, got it?"

Instead, use some of these questions. For example if you're teaching about irregular past tense verbs:

Teacher CCQ: Can you make a sentence using the past tense of "eat": (Write these words on the board as a prompt for low level students: dinner, last night, pizza.)

Student: I ate pizza for dinner last night.

Teacher CCQ: Can I you say speaked?

Student: No! Spoke!

Teacher CCQ: I ate pizza last night. Can you make it negative?

Student: I didn't eat pizza last night.

Classroom Behavior Management Strategies

Keep Emotions in Check

Never, ever let your students see you get emotional in a bad way. Of course, show your happiness or pride when they do something well! However as far as negative emotions in response to bad behaviour, try to avoid them. Their behaviour isn't about you, so don't take it personally. Easier said than done, but start by working on your poker face and a calm exterior demeanor.

We've all been there: the entire class is acting up, running around, yelling, you name it. Losing your cool will not get the class back under control.

It didn't take long for me to realize there had to be a better way. I tried several tricks from silently counting until I felt I could keep my poker face (or poker voice) to picking up my cup and going to the water fountain. Since I'm quite strict about students not leaving class, it usually had an effect if I left class. But, if your school has a policy stating teachers are required to be in the classroom if there are students present, consider using other 'cooling off' practices like breathing in for 4 beats, and out for 7 while counting those numbers—often, when a teacher stops talking for a minute it signals something is very different and students will become quiet and pay attention.

As I've said, it's better to not get to that point. Whatever it takes. Remember, too, that every class is a new beginning. You can go in to the next class and start over. It is harder, once they have an impression of you as soft on discipline or easy to rile, but it can be done.

Private Scolding is Better than Public

Don't call out students in front of their peers. No one likes to be publicly scolded. Have a quiet word outside of class. Cast it as a problem you would like to help them with, rather than behaviour that needs to be punished. ("Is there anything I can do to help you get along with So-and-so?" rather than, "Stop being such a jerk in class!") This may sound a bit glib, but really, reframing a negative behaviour can be very helpful. At the very least, it shows that you are trying to see their side, since they are unlikely to consider themselves to be in the wrong.

Practice Positive Reinforcement

Point out good behaviour at least as often as bad. When you see two students working enthusiastically on an assignment, give them a little shout out. Find something to compliment the lower achievers on. The superstars get positive reinforcement all day. Don't set the bar too low, but if you look for the good, you can usually find some.

Recognize Teacher Caused Behavioural Issues and Stop Them

Realize that student misbehaviour may be personal—there are a few things you could be doing wrong, such as:

Giving Instructions too Early

Starting to give instructions before the class is ready to listen is one common problem. This is critical in an ESL class because comprehension is already difficult enough so be sure that all your students are listening and looking at you before beginning. Some teachers use a bell to signal they're about to speak, especially with high energy and noisy classes.

Another technique for getting attention is to put your hand in the air and say "Be quiet, please" in your normal volume teacher voice (don't yell, it tires out your voice and is counter-productive) and then count down 5-4-3-2-1 as your fingers fold into your palm with each number—this allows students to finish talking or doing something and then focus their attention on the teacher. It also helps beginner level students who may not know what you said in English, but will quickly pick up on your arm up in the air and fingers counting down as a signal to pay attention and stop talking.

Not Doing a Demo

One very common problem with instructions is not doing a demonstration along with them for the students. My general rule is that I'll almost always do a demo for things that involve more than one step unless my students are absolute beginners. For example, most students can handle the instruction, "Open your book to page seven" without a demo. However, even very advanced learners will benefit from a quick demo before doing a survey activity or playing a board game for example because these things involve a number of different steps to them.

Not Giving a Visual for Instructions

When someone is speaking in another language that we're not fluent in, it can sometimes sound like, "Blah blah blah blah blah pencil blah blah paper." If this is a teacher giving instructions to their students, it's no wonder that they have a difficult time doing the activity at the end of that! Students may certainly want to do it but lack knowledge for how to complete it.

A solution to this is write down the steps in very simple language on the board or PowerPoint. Underline key words or change the color of them. Almost all language learners are able to process things written down more easily than things spoken to them.

Other Problems with Instructions

Only giving verbal instructions, giving too many instructions at once, addressing the class while your back is turned (while writing on the board, for example), speaking too quickly or with too high-level vocabulary, and/or finishing up with, "Everybody got that?" are all common problems with giving instructions.

Also, don't forget your ICQs (instruction checking questions). For example:

- How many students are in a group?
- How many minutes do you have to play?
- What is student A doing? Student B? Student C?
- What should you do when you're done?

For ICQs, I generally avoid yes/no questions and instead prefer open-ended ones.

Paying Attention to the Class Clown

Indulging the class clowns, who then don't know when to stop, because you've blurred the line between teacher and friend can cause problems in class. There are many strategies you can use to 'neutralize' a class clown:

- Move their desk to sit adjacent to the teacher's desk or put them in the front row center desk so that your proximity to them makes it easier to manage their behavior.
- Make them into a 'teaching assistant' and give them tasks to keep them focused on productive behaviors.
- Get to know them as best as you can in order to know what motivates them—this can open up behavior modification options that otherwise you might not be aware of, and build a positive teacher-student relationship as well.

Having too Many Rules

The more rules, the more you turn into a cop and need to spend a lot of time enforcing them. Of course, you need standards, but you also have to balance enforcement with getting anything else done. That said, some rules are often necessary to ensure that things run smoothly. Here are a few simple ones that you might consider using in your classes:

- Only one person talking at a time (either the teacher or a student) and everyone else is listening.
- Cell phones are only for dictionaries, not playing games or texting with friends.
- Something related to being late (depends strongly on your school's policies).
- Have a name-tag (I teach a lot of students and require that students have them on their desks for each class).
- Bring your book to class, along with a pen or pencil and notebook.
- Be kind. Everyone is trying their best to improve their English skills!

Not Looking the Part

Look at the other teachers in your school. How are they dressed? Compare that to your usual school clothes. If everyone is wearing business attire, and you look like you could go straight to a second job at a car wash, that could be part of the problem. I know wearing dry clean only clothes is an expensive hassle, but you need to look like a professional, if you want to be treated as one. Personal grooming is also important. Showing up with 'bed-head' and being unshaven, etc., may give an unintended message to students about your expectations for behavior in the classroom.

Avoid Dead-Time

Avoiding dead-time requires some organization but it's reasonably easy to do. I will never, ever write more than a few words on the board while the students are waiting. I come early and try to write most of the text I'm using for that class before they get there.

This means I usually do the grammar/vocabulary stage first or second in my lesson plan. Or, if I do it in the middle, I'll get the students working on something and then do my writing on the board. Dead-time can be hard to recover from because your students lose their focus.

Better yet, just use a simple PPT if your classrooms have computer consoles. I use Google Drive for mine.

Don't Forget about Eye Contact and Pay Attention to Dead Spots

Try to scan the entire class within a 20 second period of talking, so you'll make eye contact with each student three times in one minute. Most teachers have a dead-spot that they just don't look at for some reason. For me, it's usually the first and second rows on the right and so I make a conscious effort to fight against this every class.

Tips for Gaining Respect of the Students after You've Lost It

It is very difficult to get stricter after you have started a semester or your students have gotten to know you. The best thing to do is start hard and then soften up over time. However, since you can't go back in time with your current students, you'll just have to make the best of it. Don't worry, it can be done though.

This may seem a bit manipulative but usually the most out of control students are the ones you rarely see and whose names you don't know. So, get to know them. Make a point of arriving a few minutes early so you can chat with one or two students. Single out a few instigators before class and ask if they can help you that day—collecting notebooks or passing out game boards, whatever.

Another trick is to have students make name cards with their student numbers. They should be required to bring them to class and always have them visible on their desks. This is immensely helpful for the teacher to learn names, and if necessary make a note about a student's bad behavior (and GOOD TOO!) in order to deduct (or return points for improvement in behavior) participation points from the final grade. A class seating chart is also an option but this requires students to sit in the same place every class as well as in-class time to fill it out. Whatever you choose, the less anonymous they feel, the less likely they are to go wild.

I won't sugar coat it. You have to play the long game if the class is out of control. Just keep at it. Treat your students politely, modelling the behavior you want to see from them. Apply your rules consistently. If there is the possibility they can get away with something, many students will take those odds.

If your class is out of control, there are a few things you might want to consider. Do you have a well-planned and organized lesson prepared each day? If you waste time fumbling around searching for the things you need, they will fill the gap you've created.

Do you have activities for early finishers? Students sitting around with nothing to do will find something to do. Do you have clear rules which you apply evenly? Do you have a technique for getting attention? Do you wait for their attention before giving instructions? Are your instructions clear? Do you check their comprehension? Do you check that they are carrying out your instructions? Do you have low-key responses to misbehaviour (look, pause, comment, proximity)?

Tips for Helping Students who are Reluctant to Participate in Class

Often when students don't want to participate, it's because their language skills are far below that of their classmates. I try to coax them into the lesson in a variety of ways. Here are some of the things that I've used successfully in the past.

1. Change where the student sits, and with who—often, students enable bad behaviors in each other. Move the student to the front of the class and separate them from their friends. If their behavior improves, consider letting them return to sit with friends. NOTE: carefully consider doing this when teaching adults in university because students may become vindictive and give extremely bad reviews at the end of the semester.

2. Avoid language tasks that may embarrass the students by always giving practice time before language performance tasks. Also allow students to use scripts if they need them when doing dialogues and for communicative tasks. Consider 'mask' like puppets to give students the illusion of anonymity and being 'hidden' from view.

3. Find out if there are external events that may impact student motivation and energy levels like field trips, huge assignments in other courses or classes, etc. and adjust your expectations and the lesson/course objectives if necessary.

4. Consider whether or not a student might have a learning disability or some kind of psychological disorder like anxiety/panic attacks—their refusal to participate may have nothing to do with a bad attitude and be about something that they don't wish to disclose to you and their class mates.

5. Ask other teachers what their classroom rules and management strategies are—sometimes it may be the case that your expectations and how you run your classroom are quite different than the majority of the teachers in your school which can lead to students' routines and habits being challenged without the teacher knowing that's what is happening

If the same student is refusing to participate over and over, talk to them. Find out how they are feeling. Get to know some of their interests and try to incorporate them into activities. It can be difficult if you are teaching large classes and only see each group once or twice a week but a little personal attention goes a long way.

I had some students at one school who were far below most of their classmates and just wanted to play games on their phones. So, I found a few PowerPoint games online which were modelled after some popular games.

Any time you are dealing with a difficult student, put yourself in their shoes and think about why they are acting a certain way. It probably isn't just to disrupt class. There's likely a reason that you can hopefully address.

Tips for Lesson Planning

Assess the Level of your Students

When teaching English, it's vital to check on the ability level of the students. After all, if the lesson is too easy, then students aren't going to get as much out of the lesson as they could. If it's too difficult, they will likely feel quite frustrated and may just feel like giving up. Both of these situations should be avoided!

In terms of how to assess students' English abilities, there are a number of options. The first is if you're using a textbook put out by one of the big publishers. There is often an accompanying placement test, either on paper or online. If all students have taken an English proficiency test of some kind like the TOEFL, looking at their scores can give a pretty good indication of their level, although this is sometimes more an indication of who is good at taking tests rather than actual language ability. Talking to previous teachers at your school can give a rough estimate as well.

However, my preferred option is to generally administer my own quick assessment on the first day of class. What's on it depends on the kind of class I'm teaching. For example, if I'm teaching writing, then the assessment would consist of a writing task of some kind. If a TOEIC speaking class, then I'll find a simple online practice for TOEIC speaking to administer.

However, for general English classes with beginner to intermediate students, you might consider making up a simple 1-2 page proficiency test. Some things to test students on could include:

- writing out numbers (spelling)

- days of the week and months of the year

- simple short answer questions

- a paragraph writing task (favourite movie for example)
- a listening section where you say a question and then students have to write their answer to it
- a simple reading passage with some true/false questions

The diagnostic tool provides an enormous amount of information that saves the teacher from having to try to talk one to one with each student in every class. I tell students not to worry about finishing if they can't because it's not graded. And if the majority of students in a class can't finish the test—that gives me a clear indication that it's a low level class.

I typically give this test in the first class after doing my intro PPT of myself, an ice-breaking activity, classroom rules, course objectives/assignments/exams, and then the last part of the class is for the assessment. I don't grade it but I do look over every paper so that I get a general sense of the class level.

Fail to Plan = Plan to Fail

When teaching the same material over and over from semester to semester, it can be very tempting to roll into class and wing it. After all, we could teach the lesson in our sleep, right? Actually, it may be possible to get away with it once or twice but students can see lack of preparation from a mile away. If we don't care about planning a lesson, why should the students care about our class?

I'm not saying you need to create a multi-page, minute-by-minute plan for every class, no matter how many times you've taught the same lesson. Keep in mind that each class is different, even if the material isn't. Tailoring the lesson, even just a bit to each individual class will keep it a little bit fresher for you too.

Over-Planning is Better than Under-Planning

I'll be the first to admit I don't always fill in a complete lesson plan, particularly when teaching the same material for the 100th time, but in my early days of teaching, it made a massive difference. It helped not only with the above-mentioned points, but also boosted my confidence and prevented me from trying to teach the entire language in one day.

Over-planning is a good way to make sure you have enough material, in case your lesson is easier than you expect. However, just because there's a lot in the lesson doesn't mean you need to rush to get it all in. Expect that the last couple of things will only be gotten to if required.

Use at Least a Basic Lesson Plan

If you're a little shaky on how to plan an ESL/EFL lesson, consider following this basic guide. Each section of this book (tips for teaching reading/speaking/writing/reading/grammar) will have more details about teaching that specific kind of lesson so be sure to check those out as well.

1. **SWBAT**: By the end of the lesson, Students Will Be Able To _____. What is the learning outcome of this lesson? For example, by the end of this lesson, students will be able to ask and answer questions about food and drink which they like and don't like.

2. **Language focus:** To continue with the above example, the grammar pattern will be subject + like/don't like + object. The vocabulary will be names of foods and drinks. Your lesson plan should list exactly which terms you are covering. This is especially helpful if you are teaching classes of different levels to keep you from getting them confused.

3. **Warm up:** Don't just dive into the heart of the lesson. Review what was covered in the previous lesson, or have a fun (quick) activity to orient the students to using English.

4. **Presentation:** Here you will introduce the new language and grammar and provide examples demonstrating how to use it correctly. If there is a dialogue in the textbook, this is the ideal time to use it.

5. **Practice:** In this part of the lesson, students will have very controlled practice using the

new language. You should have a couple of activities allowing them to move from "repeat after me" (presentation) to using the language themselves (production). This includes such activities as dialogues with parts removed, so they have to listen to their partner and respond appropriately.

6. **Production:** In the final part of the lesson, students demonstrate their comprehension of the lesson by using the target language to speak or write. This includes activities like making a dialogue with a partner or a short writing task.

7. **Conclusion:** For me, this means it's time for a game which focuses on the target language. This allows the students further opportunities for using the target language while having some fun. Other ideas for wrapping up include a brief discussion related to the lesson.

8. **Review:** Finally, don't forget about review. Do a quick spot-check to make sure that students have gotten the key concepts from the lesson. If not, then follow-up in the next class.

Recycle Teaching Materials Whenever Possible

Hopefully you've been saving your lessons somewhere in a place like *Dropbox* or *Google Drive*. There are always plenty of common conversation topics that can be used and learned in different lesson formats where you may be free to use any lesson you wish. It's really useful to use an old lesson rather than pulling something new out of your hat.

Plus, I often teach the same English textbook semester to semester. I'll use the exact same lessons but just think back to what didn't work and adapt it a little bit. This takes 5-10 minutes, instead of an hour or two. Consider yourself fortunate if this is your situation as well and take full advantage of it!

Be Realistic about How Much Material Can be Covered

One issue new teachers often have to deal with is paring back their lessons to a realistic amount of content. For example, in a reading class, there may be four, 40-minute lessons to cover a 10-page story. Of course, it's ideal if students really understand the text.

However, a more realistic goal may be for the students to understand the gist of the material. Pre-teach the vocabulary they absolutely must know and activate their prior knowledge of the subject in some way. Pause periodically to discuss and summarize what has been read. Trying to cover every difficult word or every cultural reference before or during reading will bog your students down, bore them, and take too much class time.

The Sweet Spot

Lesson plans should hit the sweet spot of adequately covering the material and keeping the lesson moving, without trying to cram too much into one day. Since lesson plans are for your eyes only, feel free to add helpful notes to yourself. When I first started teaching elementary school students and kindergarten kids, I would sometimes forget myself and start speaking at a regular pace without adjusting my language. Little notes, like "slow down," and, "simple words," helped keep me on the right track.

Let Students Know Where they're Going

People like to know what's happening so write up a little schedule for the day on one side of the board, and leave it there for the entire class, or have it as the first slide of your PPT for students to see before class starts.

Tips for Giving Homework

Giving (or not giving) homework may be something which your school dictates, but if you do give homework, here are a couple of suggestions.

Make it Relevant

Don't give your students random worksheets or other assignments which bear little relation to the lesson they have learned.

If you Assign it, Check it

This can be as simple as putting a "Good work!" stamp at the top of the page. If you ask your students to take the time to do the work, it is the least you can do. If it isn't important enough to check, why should they do it? No one likes busy work. If your students get the feeling you are giving them busy work, they will be resentful.

Stop the Homework Madness, Part 1

One of the biggest time-savers, or time-suckers for teachers is homework! If it's a conversation class, one idea is to get the students to make videos, either just talking by themselves or interviewing someone. Then, have them put the videos on *YouTube* and email you the link. It's far easier than dealing with stacks of paperwork, and the other bonus is that it practices speaking in a speaking class.

If a student meets the basic requirements as set out in the assignment, I give them full points. However, I also offer some very specific feedback for errors students may be making when speaking.

Stop the Homework Madness, Part 2

Another form of homework madness is in writing classes. I've taught advanced academic writing a few times where students are writing 5-paragraph academic essays. Forms of madness for a class like this involve:

- getting nitty-gritty into every single grammatical mistake
- requiring students to submit endless revisions
- attempting any sort of "group" essay writing
- weekly assignments

For writing, I choose to focus on the big picture things like thesis statements + topic sentences, logical arguments and cohesive devices.

Endless revisions sent to me by email are my personal form of hell. Instead, I do some serious "self-editing" in class. It's better for the students too! I won't be there to hold their hand once they graduate and have a job where they have to write in English. Here are a couple of checklists to consider adapting for your own purposes:

Self-Editing Checklist for Basic Punctuation

- Check every first word of a sentence has a capital
- Check all proper nouns have capitals
- Check that all sentences have a period and space before the next sentence
- Check that the first sentence of each paragraph is indented
- Make sure you don't cut words at the end of a line when they are only one syllable, and for words that are multi-syllabic make sure you don't randomly cut them in the middle of a syllable

Self-Editing Checklist for an Opinion Essay

- Do you have a good hook/opening sentence that grabs the reader's attention?
- Is your opinion/thesis sentence answering the essay question?
- Do you have 2-3 sentences that preview the supporting premises?
- Do each of your main body paragraphs have a clear topic sentence that states each supporting reason/premise?
- Do you give supporting details in each of the main body paragraphs? Are there facts and examples given that support the topic sentence of each paragraph?
- Do you have a conclusion sentence in each main body paragraph that also links to the next paragraph?
- Does your conclusion paragraph re-state your thesis?
- Do you summarize your supporting reasons?
- Do you have a final thought sentence that leaves the reader with a sense of the overall message of the essay?

Tips for What to Do After a Terrible Lesson

So you've just had a terrible lesson where everything seemed to go wrong. The first thing to keep in mind is to not panic or beat yourself up. Regardless of how you screwed up, if no one was physically or emotionally harmed, everything will be alright.

Teachers are just as human as everyone else. We make mistakes and have bad days. Everyone recovers, even the students who have had to suffer through a terrible lesson with a teacher on the verge of a nervous breakdown.

If the mistake was with your planning, learn from it. Make a note of what went right and what went wrong and try to minimize the "what went wrong" part of each lesson. You can do this by putting more effort into your planning, asking colleagues for advice, looking online for ideas, or professional development to up your game in the long term. There is a vast expanse of information out there to make use of.

You may also want to invest in some EFL/ESL teaching methodology books like Jeremy Harmer's "The Practice of English Language Teaching." This is generally considered to be the "Bible" of EFL/ESL teaching. There is a smaller version, "How to Teach English," by Harmer that is a much easier and faster to read text. Scott Thornbury has a series of "How to Teach _____" (grammar, speaking, vocabulary) books that are great too.

If the mistake was more along the lines of behaviour management, like shouting at the class or berating a student, that is fixable too. Reflect on what happened to get you into that state and think about how you can avoid it in the future. Find a way to keep calm in class, no matter what the students are doing to push your buttons.

Over time, I realized that all aspects of the classroom, not just methodology or materials, need continual assessment and refinement. I also lost my fear of changing the rules mid way through a course. That's not to say I make changes on a whim or try every flavour of the month; I just keep track of what I'm doing and how the students respond to it.

Tips for Dealing with Terrible Textbooks

Don't use it. Unfortunately, I know, that's usually not an option. The students have already paid for it! That's okay. You can visibly use parts of each chapter and supplement it with related but useful materials. Look critically at each lesson for something salvageable: theme, vocabulary, grammar, etc. Take what you can use and find or create related materials to go along with that. If the dialogues are riddles with errors, create your own as a model, and have students make and perform dialogues. If the activities are too easy or difficult, modify them accordingly. As long as your students are opening their books each class and writing something in them sometimes, you are "using the book."

I've been given a lot of garbage to work with, but I've never been taken to task for adding to it. As long as I followed the expected time frame and taught the vocabulary and grammar presented, at least loosely, no one ever noticed that's all I was using the book for. As with so many things, appearances count. It is usually enough just to look like you are using the required textbook.

Consider Using Warm-Ups

You are probably well aware that a warm-up is a short activity used at the start of class but you may think it is a waste of valuable class time. It's not! Many of your students will not have spoken English or even given it a single thought since you last saw them.

With just a bit of planning, a warm-up can review a previous lesson or recycle older material to refresh your students' memory. It can also preview a new topic. Based on the students' performance with the warm-up, it's possible to mentally adjust the lesson, if necessary, rather than change track once having gotten started.

In this way, warm-ups aren't just good for students, they are good for teachers as well as an informal assessment tool. How well have the students retained that lesson? Are there any apparent gaps in their understanding? Did that student who got 100% on last week's quiz seem to have forgotten everything? Tests only tell part of the story so take advantage of informal assessment opportunities whenever possible.

Here are two resources that can easily be found on *Amazon*:

39 ESL Warm-Ups for Kids

39 ESL Warm-Ups for Teenagers and Adults

More Reasons to Use ESL Warm-Up Activities

There are a number of other reasons why you might consider using an ESL warm-up game or activity in your classes. Here are a few of the most important ones:

- They can activate students' prior knowledge about a topic, grammar point or vocabulary set.

- They can engage the learners from the start of the lesson and help them learn English.

- Warm-ups can help to ease students into learning English. If you just dive right into the heart of the lesson, the important things can be missed.

- ESL warm-ups are an ideal way to review material from previous classes.

- They help to build rapport between students and teachers.

- Depending on what you do, they can be quite enjoyable and fun for the students.

Lone Ranger all the Way for Lesson Planning!

Some teachers are all about collaboration. I love the idea, in theory. But, my experience with it has been that it ends up sucking up ridiculous amounts of time. Everyone has their own way of doing things, and of course, my way is the best way! Just joking about this, but only kind of!

Although shared tests or lesson planning probably result in better tests or lesson plans, it's often going to use up a lot more time than just planning your own lesson.

One alternative to requiring teachers to all use the same lesson PLAN is to collectively make the same learning objectives and related content. For example, make a list of speaking objectives, skills, strategies, vocabulary, grammar, and cultural content that students must learn and be able to use by the end of a semester. If possible, make brief descriptions of how testing formats and assignments will be done, rubrics, and how much of the final grade is given to each item. Then allow teachers to deliver/teach those things according to their individual personalities, teaching practices, training, and experience. This will usually result in a much happier teaching environment.

Just about the only exception to this is when using something like *Breaking News English*. They have longer, very detailed full lesson plans and then mini 2-page ones that are excellent. It's easy to just print these off and use them almost without changing anything.

Appropriate Language

Over the years, I've seen plenty of teachers interact with their students. Some certainly use language at an appropriate level that the students are able to mostly understand. However, there are also plenty of teachers who speak far too quickly and use far too complicated grammatical constructions and advanced vocabulary.

What's the reaction of the students with the latter? Like deer in the headlights. No sort of comprehension or understanding and just nervous laughter in response. While some people say, "It's the real world and they should just get used to it," I tend to disagree. Learning a language is a process and while advanced students might need this, beginners and intermediate students often aren't at a level where they're able to handle it well. There are two main ways that you might consider adjusting your language: speed and difficulty, or a combination of the two.

#1. Speed

Use whatever grammar or vocabulary you want but speak more slowly. Also use pauses to allow for some thinking and processing time. The lower the level, the slower you should talk. For advanced students, a normal speaking speed will be appropriate.

#2. Difficulty, in Terms of Grammar/Vocabulary

Make it simpler for lower-level students and more difficult for higher-level ones. However, avoid doing what some foreign teachers do and drop articles or use incorrect grammar. This does not help our students!

Tips for Beginning a Class

Over the years, I've kind of struggled with how to begin an English class. Not the very first class but all the other ones after that. If you're in the same boat, keep on reading. I'll share my top tips with you about how to begin your English classes in style.

I know everyone has their own way to start a class but here's what I do. I try to arrive early so I don't have to do all this stuff while students are attentively watching and waiting for me! A requirement I have is that students talk to me after class, instead of before because I have more time to help them.

#1: Check the Classroom Environment

I walk into the class, adjust the temperature, desks and podium to my liking. I'll turn on the computer and projector if I'm using it for that class. I say a few random hellos as students walk in. Remember: you are the teacher and it's up to you to make a comfortable learning environment. Something like opening the blinds to allow a little natural light can really make a big difference. Or, making sure that the blinds are closed if the sun is shining directly onto the PowerPoint screen.

#2: Prepare Materials

I take my stuff out of my bag and set out all the materials I'll need for that class. There is nothing worse than having students' attention and losing it due to poor preparation and having to search in your bag for things.

#3: Write the Day's Agenda on the Board

I write up the day's agenda on the board or load up the PowerPoint that has it. I'll also write the first one or two things that we'll be doing on the board so I don't waste class time doing this later. By this time, there is usually about a couple of minutes until class starts so I'll walk around doing attendance.

#4: General Chit-Chat and an ESL Warm-Up Activity

I'll start with a good afternoon/morning and then some general chit-chat for a couple minutes. I'll avoid this with the really quiet classes because dead silence is never a good start to a class but it's actually quite fun with the more outgoing ones. I like to find out what's going on in my students' lives!

Then, I get into a quick warm-up activity or game.

Tips for Teaching English to Teenage or Adult Beginners

Teach a Few Things, a Lot

It's better that beginners take away a few things with them from class that they know really well, instead of a ton of things that they don't really know at all. Keep this in mind and avoid the temptation to power through a textbook just for the sake of it.

One particular area where this is particularly relevant is with vocabulary. For absolute beginners, even five new words can be challenging while students at a slightly higher level may be able to handle ten new words per lesson. As a general rule, the absolute maximum for number of new words to introduce in a single lesson is fifteen.

It's All About Review

Teaching English to beginners is ALL about review. I like to incorporate it a few ways into my classes. First is at the end of class. Second is at the beginning of a class for things previously studied. Finally, I dedicate a class or two to it before any sort of exam. Check out these books on *Amazon* for practical ideas on how to do this:

39 ESL Review Games and Activities for Teenagers and Adults

39 ESL Review Games and Activities for Kids

Consider Topics Carefully

Just because your students are at a beginner level, it doesn't mean that you should treat them like children. One key area related to this is topic selection. They usually don't want to study about animals, colors, etc. like little kids would!

Be creative, however, when teaching elementary aka beginner level language content. Teens and young adults love card games. For example, Uno" has numbers, colors, and verbs. Make a rule requiring students to say out loud the card they are playing's color, action (e.g. "pick up 2"), and other game English expressions that are also used in every day spoken English (Hurry up! What did you say? Who's turn is it? Why did you do that?!).

When teaching the English names of colours, you might try doing a fashion-themed lesson with major brand names that require the language objective "Q: What's your favorite color to wear? A: I like to wear _____ (color) _____ (clothing brand name) _____ (article of clothing)."Lastly, with animals, you might try a creative lesson in which students learn verbs and "Q: What can it/he/she do? A: It/He/She can _____." Show them a video clip of a popular movie like "Fantastic Beasts and Where to Find Them." This will stimulate their imaginations, and hopefully pre-empt any protests that students are being asked to do something 'childish.'

Keep these things in mind during lesson planning. It's definitely possible to find articles with simple grammar and vocabulary that aren't written for little kids.

One easy way to increase motivation for this group of students is to find out what their favourite pop culture things are, including celebrities, singers, movies, etc. Then, try to incorporate some of these things into lessons. The language of the lesson may not be familiar but the content will be which can make it easier.

Avoid Surprises in the ESL Classroom

Adults often don't like tasks that put them on the spot in front of their peers. Use a variety of activities and games but try to avoid ever putting anyone in the spotlight. Give students thinking time or have them compare with a partner before having to say something in front of the entire class.

However, each day should be a little bit different so things don't get stale and boring. There are a ton of ESL activities for adult beginners, so get creative. Try to do at least one "fun" thing each class, along with a mix of more serious things.

Another way to mix things up is to use a variety of lesson types. Some lessons could focus on speaking or conversation, while others focus on reading, writing or listening. Have a party day and play some fun games or consider an activity that gets students doing something fun outside, while using English.

Ask Students if they Want Homework

Adults usually have very different expectations about things like homework when they're studying English. Some will expect it, while others won't. Ask your students what they want and they'll usually tell you! They may also have some very specific ideas of things they want to do. Some ideas are the following:

- Writing an essay or other kind of writing

- Preparing a resume or cover letter in English

- Reading a simple English novel or graded reader

- Recording themselves saying something

- Preparing an English speech

- Etc.

Ask for Feedback and Be Willing to Adapt

Your adult students will often have some excellent feedback for you in terms of how the class is going so please ask them. I generally do this on the midterm exam with this question: What's your favourite thing we've done so far? What's one thing you didn't like about this class?

Of course, I read the answers carefully and if I see the same thing more than once, I'll know it's something I need to consider changing. You might also consider doing an online survey—and give 5 points on the mid-term, and 5 points on the final exam for doing it. There are free online survey sites (surveymonkey.com) that you can use.

Offer Lots of Encouragement and Praise

Yes, adults love positive words or encouragement during the learning process. Be positive and upbeat, as well as kind and gentle in correcting errors. There are many different ways to reward good behaviour. Here are just a few examples.

1. **Class "Dollars."** Print off class dollars that students can use once a month, for example, to 'purchase' inexpensive prizes that are also age appropriate and desirable

2. **Combine giving praise with teaching new English vocabulary/expressions**. Some examples include a) Groovy, baby! b) Unbelievable! c) That was out of this world! d) Fantabulous! (fantastic + fabulous)—advanced students will EAT THIS UP!

3. **Win Lunch with the Teacher.** This shouldn't only be based on whichever student gets the highest score on a test or assignment, or who talks the most in class. Alternative categories can be: a) Most improved academic ability, b) Always on time and prepared, or c) Best helper to other students.

Remember that Students are Good at Other Things

Just because a student isn't that good at English, doesn't mean that they're not a pro at something else or a number of other things. Maybe you can even learn something from them? Be curious and find out!

When asking students to do a presentation, allow them to choose a topic that they love; this can be made easier for low level language learners by encouraging them to use pictures they take with their phone, short videos, or realia--real world objects. For example, if they study how to play the kayageum ("traditional Korean zither-like string instrument with 12 strings") or Taekwondo (Korean martial art) they can bring different props to use while making a presentation.

All About Teaching Writing to ESL Beginners

Teaching beginners to write in English can be a very difficult job. These students often struggle to put together a sentence so teaching them to "write" can be quite overwhelming. Many teachers instead find themselves just focusing on students' grammar mistakes. This isn't a terrible thing but then it kind of becomes a grammar class instead of one focused on writing.

Before we get into specific tips, be sure to keep this overall thought in mind. During my CELTA course, my tutor pointed out that writing is any time students pick up a pen or pencil and write something. It can be as simple as filling in a blank with one word and it certainly doesn't have to be a formal essay or something like that. Beyond that, here are a number of tips that you might consider using.

If you have to start with learning how to print the upper and lower case alphabet letters, do it; trying to read horribly illegible printing causes too many problems: in-class peer editing becomes very difficult, marking tests will become intolerably stressful and take a lot of time for the teacher, and on external exams like IELTS they will lose many points if the writing is illegible

In terms of sentence length, explicitly tell students to keep the number of words to a 3-5 word range/maximum, this helps to avoid making students feel like they have to write long and complex sentences.

Make a color code for different parts of speech: blue for nouns, green for verbs, etc. use this when writing on the whiteboard with colored markers (if time permits), and in PowerPoint slides you can color code key words in a text—this helps students associate the color with the part of speech, and is a sub-channel of visual information processing, which has become a dominant learning style in our social media cultures

Another strategy is to make worksheets with writing exercises that have writing prompts and word banks.

Example 1—Fill in the blanks:

Q: _____ (How/Why) are you today? A: I'm _____ (Friday, good).

Example 2—Correct the punctuation:

    i like icecream   I like icecream.

    it is delicious   It is delicious.

    my favorite is chocolate   My favorite is chocolate.

Example 3—Write a creative poem:

Step 1: Write 3 category titles on the board: Colours Verbs Nouns

Step 2: Elicit colours, verbs, and nouns from students. Ask them which category the word should be written under.

Step 3: Make 3 lines as a model for students.

Colour	Verb	Noun
red	flying	father
green	jumping	mother
blue	eating	brother

Step 4: You can add elements of creativity for students to mimic like: make the letters of "flying" look like they're flying, or add wings to one or more of the letters, use markers that are colours of the words, and choose one letter of the nouns and modify it to be a stick figure drawing of a father, or whatever the noun might be (e.g. airplane)

Example-1st, Production-2nd

For beginners, it really is all about examples first and production second so help your students out by giving them something solid to grasp onto. Most beginning students can partially copy what's on the board and then adapt it to make it true for them. This isn't a bad thing if that's where students are at in terms of ability.

Use this Beginner Writing Textbook

If you're teaching an intensive writing class (and not just doing writing as part of a 4-skills class) and are looking for a beginner level ESL writing textbook for high school students or adults, my top recommendation is *Great Writing 1: Great Sentences for Great Paragraphs* by Keith Folse (easily found on *Amazon*). It focuses on the sentence and paragraph level, which will be challenging enough for beginner English students.

Trust me, there are lots of books out there but none are better than this one if you want to focus specifically on writing. It has a nice blend of process and product approaches to teaching writing. Students learn how to do things like editing, use varied vocabulary, etc. They also study the finished product and have to replicate it for themselves.

Tips for Avoiding the English Teacher Burnout Thing

You know that feeling when you teach the simple past for the 57th time or that unit in the book about hobbies or chores for the 32nd time? Or the students who email you asking for a higher grade when they've done nothing to deserve it and their email is copied straight from Google translate? Or admin who tell you some vitally important thing at the very last second and then get annoyed that you didn't know about it sooner?

These things can add up and you'll find yourself a pretty unhappy ESL/EFL teacher in no time. But, here are a few tips that helped me get through a decade teaching English in Korea. Believe it or not, I was positive and upbeat almost the entire time.

Look after Yourself

To avoid being burnt out, looking after your health is key. This involves getting enough sleep, drinking only in moderation, exercising and eating healthy food. A full day of teaching on a hangover or with a bad cold can be extremely difficult and lead to a whole bunch of unhappiness. Getting enough sleep every night is also important—you can't be healthy and teach well after a late night, or series of nights out drinking and going to sleep at 4am.

Teaching English isn't exactly difficult in terms of brainpower required but it can be hard with lots of teaching hours if you aren't in top condition with lots of energy to face the day.

Just Use the Textbook!

Most textbooks have at least a few good pages in them. Use them for most of the class and then, if necessary, put time and effort into making up one fabulous extra activity. Don't even think about doing more than one of these supplemental things for each class if you're feeling sapped of energy and heading towards burnout.

It takes too much time and your goal should be to plan lessons that are as awesome as possible in the shortest amount of time. A ton of lesson planning hours does not always equal better lessons.

Also remember to keep track of your lesson plans and extra games or activities in *Google Drive* or *DropBox* so you can recycle them with different classes or if you end up teaching the same course again. And no, you're not a bad teacher for using the book. You're just a smart one.

For Tests, Simple is Best!

I have some colleagues who record speaking tests and go back and listen to them later on to grade them. This is double the amount of work I want to do! Plus, it's the worst kind of busy work—extremely boring and tedious. I listen and grade at the same time while students are speaking to each other and find it easy enough. The key is to have students talk to each other, instead of you because it can be quite difficult to keep the conversation going and evaluate at the same time. That said, it can be helpful to record students on speaking tests just in case you need to refer back to them for some reason. However, don't make it a point to not evaluate them the first time round, when students are actually speaking.

Another tip is to make the test out of the same number of points as the total percentage. For example, if my final is worth 30% of the final grade, I'll make the test out of 30 points, with each question being worth one point. If homework is worth 6%, I'll grade it out of six points. This saves me an extra step at the end because I don't have to convert things.

When grading, I also do the all or nothing. Adding up 1/2 points here and there is another one of my personal hells. By using the all or nothing method, I can grade each midterm or final exam in less than a minute (a grammar/vocabulary test, essays obviously take much longer to grade).

Learn to Say No

Teachers always get asked to do lots of stuff that is not really part of our jobs. For example, some do extra teaching or go on a field trip that lasts all weekend. If you want to do it, you should. If it's reasonable and won't take up much of your time, you should also do it just to make sure things go smoothly at work. But, if it's going to take up way too much time or energy, just say no.

Don't be that pushover who gets all the stuff dumped on them that others are smart enough not to touch with a ten foot pole! Of course, you should have a good excuse like a promise with a friend or something like that. And be sure to do a stellar job at everything that is part of your job, such as lesson planning, grading, phone calls to students, etc.

Consider Overtime Carefully

I consider the overtime that I do extremely carefully. Some things just aren't worth the money if it will require a ridiculous amount of preparation because it's a "serious" class that I've never taught before. I would possibly do it if there were opportunities to do it again in the future. But, a one-off? I'll usually say no.

Private teaching with little kids? Some teachers are all about it, but this is one of my personal hells and I'll almost always say no. On the other hand, I'll usually say yes to kids' camps because I find that they're usually quite fun and there's a nice degree of freedom to teach a variety of interesting things and have lots of fun with the students.

Motivation isn't Just for the Students

When most people think of classroom motivation, they think of rewards for good behaviour but it's much more than that. It's consequences, too. I kid. I mean, we tend to spend a lot of time and effort on our students' motivation but our own can get short shrift. It's normal to go through periods when you just want the semester to be over. However, if it's only half-term, or the semester hasn't even started, you might want to give some attention to your motivation.

For me, being active in a professional organization such as *Kotesol* in Korea has been the key to staying excited about my work and keeping it fresh. I get to spend time with people who are truly passionate about education and this enthusiasm is infectious. I can remind myself why I love teaching, get new ideas and keep up to date with the latest trends in education.

On the flip side, as much as possible, I avoid teachers who hate their jobs because their negativity is also contagious. You know the ones: they complain about their students, the admin, teaching materials, class schedule, etc. You name it and they will let you know how terrible it is. Of course, the problem is never them or their attitude. I've worked at a few sketchy places with regular payday tales of woe, constantly changing schedules, no materials, etc. I know how frustrating it is but there is a line between venting and still making the best of it. Life's too short to be that person or spend too much time around them.

Other ways to stay motivated include studying for a higher degree, keeping up with the latest research and (most fun) trawling *Pinterest* for new ideas. *LinkedIn* is a great way to network, if workshops and conferences don't do it for you or if you are too busy to attend live events.

Think about Work Space

Make sure that you have a happy place where you can get work done so you can put some focused effort into stuff. For me, it's usually not at home. If I want to be productive, it's far better for me to go into my office, which I'm lucky enough to share with only 2 people who are rarely (if ever) there.

When we are there together, people just do their own thing and while friendly, we don't carry on a running conversation, thankfully. If you have chatty office mates, you may want to realize that it's not the place to do serious work.

Some people who work at other universities share an office with 10+ people and of course, serious work is often impossible in that kind of environment. So, those people could maybe find a quiet coffee shop near their house, a public library or set-up a space at home to do serious work like lesson planning and grading. Whatever works for you. Just be sure to find that space where you can focus and be sure to go there if you need to get lots of things done.

Stay on Top of the Paperwork

If you let the paperwork build up, it's going to make your life more stressful. Grade homework within a couple of days. Enter grades into your spreadsheet as soon as possible. It's better for the students too because you can let them know their current score in the class, should they want to know.

Important If you rock the paper grade sheets, as opposed to the spreadsheet, make sure you photocopy the sheets each time you add new grades. And obviously, store the original and then the photocopies separately! This way, you'll be okay in case you happen to lose your grading folder. It can happen when you move from class to class.

Keep Moving Onwards and Upwards

One of the best ways to stay motivated is to keep moving onwards and upwards in the English teaching world. I had one colleague who made it a rule to stay in the same country for only two years. By the time I met him in Korea, he'd already taught in six different places!

Also consider some moves within the same country. Perhaps you can find a job with better hours and/or more pay. Or, better students. Whatever the case, always keep your eyes open and your ear to the ground to see what else is out there.

In my own teaching career, I moved from a terrible hagwon (cram school) in Korea to a better one. Then, I got my first university job and after that, a better paying one in one of the best cities in Korea. I got a serious dose of motivation for teaching every time I made the switch!

Think about Life After Teaching

Some English teachers plan to do it forever. That's fine, but for the vast majority, teaching English is just a stepping stone on the way to do something else. If this is the case for you, then consider carefully what your plan is for after teaching. Maybe traveling for a while? Going back to school? Moving back home and getting a job?

Whatever it is, the most successful people are those who made a plan before leaving their teaching post and also those who managed to save up a bit of money for the transition. There are two books to check out on *Amazon* related to this:

Life After ESL: Foreign Teachers Returning Home

The Wealthy English Teacher

Tips for Teaching Speaking

Listening is Important Too

It's tempting, even in our first language to not listen to our conversation partner but instead think of the next witty or wise thing to say in our heads. This does not lead to good conversations. Instead, truly listen to what your partner is saying and then respond to that. I make sure to talk to my students about this because it's even more tempting to do this in a second or third language where you are struggling to put words together into coherent sentences. There are a few tips I tell my students to help them out.

The first and last words in the question are key if it is a "W/H" question. For example, "Where do you go to school?" If you hear *where*, then you know that your answer needs to be a place of some sort and if you hear school, the answer should be quite obvious.

If a student catches the key words in a question, it's possible for them to make a reasonable guess at the correct answer. This tip is also especially useful for something like the *TOEIC* listening test, where many of the possible answers can be eliminated simply by knowing what the first word in the question is.

I also teach my students phrases that they can use if they didn't understand the question and missed the key words. For example, they could say something like, "Sorry, could you please repeat the question?" or, "I didn't understand, could you say it again slowly?" I tell them that it's not a terrible thing to ask someone to repeat something and that it's always better than giving a completely random answer that's unrelated to the question.

Lessons Don't Always Need to be Fun

When you're new to teaching, there is the temptation to always be a constant entertainer. I call these people edutainers. However, edutainer mode is hard to keep up, week after week, month after month, and year after year. While it's good to have a laugh and a joke once in a while, learning English is not easy so it is okay to have more serious kinds of activities that do not involve a game of some sort.

For example, two people talking together for a few minutes about a certain topic is extremely valuable because that means that every single student in your class is either listening or talking in a very active way for the duration of that activity. It also gives students a chance to get feedback from a partner similar to their own level, which is helpful because they are able to see if what they are saying is comprehensible, or not. Students will appreciate your classes if their English speaking skills are improving, even if you are not the most entertaining teacher so don't be afraid to do some more serious things.

Change Partners Often

A common thing that happens in ESL classes is that students sit with the same partner every single day. One way that our students know they are making a mistake is if their partner is unable to understand them. If a student goes with the same partner each time, that partner will get to know their mistakes and be able to understand them, even if nobody else can which isn't useful. Another reason that you need to change it up is that students are usually more motivated to speak in the target language (English!) if they aren't with their BFF. Finally, it simply gets boring to talk to the same person over and over again so changing it up periodically will increase motivation in your classes.

Give Feedback

If you hear some errors while students are speaking, it can be helpful to give feedback to them. Think back to your own experiences of learning a language, sport skill or musical instrument. Part of learning is just practicing on your own but I'm sure there were cases when you got some extremely valuable feedback about an error you were making which accelerated your improvement significantly. Our students want us to give them feedback on the errors that they are making and in my own informal surveys that is what students think my most important role should be.

There are two schools of thought about this: error correction can happen during the activity or at the end. My general rule is that when focusing on accuracy, it is helpful to correct errors during an activity. This is especially true for the controlled practice activities. However, if focusing on fluency, correct at the end and don't interrupt.

Don't forget that it's not helpful to correct everything unless for very advanced level students. Doing so will overwhelm students and destroy their confidence. I will usually correct the following types of errors:

1. Those that impede understanding and communication in a significant way but only if it's something that my students are at a level to understand. For example, maybe a high beginner student doesn't know how to form questions and is asking, "dinner-eat?" It would be helpful to stop and at least write the correct form on the board for the student to copy, "What will _____ _____ tonight?"

2. Those that directly involve the target language of that lesson.

3. Those that involve something we recently studied together in the past month or two.

4. Those that students at their level should have down cold. For example, a high-intermediate level student should not be making any mistakes using the simple past.

Use the Whiteboard for Key Words and Phrases

Just because you showed your students some vocabulary or a new grammar concept once or twice doesn't mean that they're going to remember it or be able to recall it when necessary. A way that we can help them is by writing the key vocabulary words or phrases that you are studying that day on one side of the whiteboard and leave them up there for the entire class to refer to if necessary. This is especially important for beginners because they often don't have the scaffolding in place in their brains to connect new material to, as our more advanced level students would. Gradually, as students become more proficient at using those particular words or grammatical constructs, we can stop putting them on the board and challenge students to recall them on their own.

Change Up Activities Frequently

Just because you did a speaking game or activity that worked well one class doesn't mean that you should keep using it again and again. This will become boring really quickly. Variety is key to keeping our students interested and engaged in the class and it's always good to challenge our students with new things so that they can improve their skills.

There are two books to check out on *Amazon* that are filled with student-centered, engaging and interactive games and activities:

101 ESL Activities for Teenagers and Adults

101 ESL Activities for Kids

Or, consider checking out my website www.eslactivity.org for dozens of ideas of things you can do in class.

Repetition is Key

Be sure to provide plenty of opportunities for students to practice. Start out with controlled practice and then move to freer speaking sessions where students can experiment with using the language. Then, follow up with review in subsequent classes.

Another thing to think about is teaching language in "chunks." If students can get to the point where these things become automatic, they'll be well on their way to becoming fluent in English.

See Scott Thornbury's: *How to Teach Speaking*, Chapter 2 for more details on "chunks" or multi-word units. Here are some examples that he mentions:

- Collocations (rich and famous)
- Idioms (cool as a cucumber)
- Phrasal verbs (log out)
- Sentence frames (would you like a . . .)
- Discourse markers (by the way)

Keep Fluency + Accuracy in Balance

In years gone by, it was all about accuracy when speaking and in places like Korea, it's still predominant with the use of things like the Audio Lingual and Grammar Translation approaches in public education.

Many teachers revert to this as well simply because it's easier to pick out errors in pronunciation, vocabulary or grammar and then correct them than it is to help students speak more quickly.

However, there has been a radical shift in thinking in the past few years and there is now a focus on fluency before grammatical accuracy. It's how we learn our first language when we're young. We utter things, fluently, that actually make no grammatical sense but grammatical accuracy comes later.

Tips for Teaching Low Level Speaking Classes

I really get how difficult it can be to teach "conversation" classes to very low level students who can barely say their name or what they ate for dinner last night—we've all been there. Then there are the expectations of the parents, our bosses, and the students themselves that we are supposed to perform a miracle of sorts and turn these very low level students into fluent English speakers who are comfortable conversing in English over the course of a single semester.

To make matters worse, we often only see our students for two or three hours a week, if that and in a class of ten or more. It's very unrealistic but unfortunately, it's the situation that we often find ourselves in. Here are a few tips for dealing with this.

Don't Hope for Miracles

Just because your boss, the students and the parents unrealistically expect miracles from you, doesn't mean that you need to as well. Be gentle with yourself and of course sincerely try to help your students improve their English speaking skills, but in the end it is up to the students to either take what you give them and run with it, or not.

If not, there isn't much you can do besides continue to do your best to inspire and motivate. Certainly don't lose any sleep over it. I've had plenty of students in South Korean universities, who, despite having had studied English for ten years or more couldn't even tell me their name or what city they were from. I knew that simply getting that student to be able to tell me these things by the end of the semester would be a big improvement, even if they weren't speaking in a full sentence.

When you're teaching beginners in speaking classes, celebrate the little improvements that you see and focus on those things. For example, the student who struggled with pronouncing a word correctly but finally got it. Cherish the moment when a student says something besides, "I'm fine, thank you, and you?" in response to your, "How are you today?"

Or the student who had been struggling in a previous lesson but then is able to answer your review question at the beginning of the next class. Enjoy the feeling when one of the very shy students talks to you in the few minutes before class starts. There are plenty of little things in the stages before a "real conversation" that you can celebrate.

Focus on Other Skills First

One of the theories of language learning is that a solid foundation in the more passive skills (listening and reading) comes before the more active production skills (writing and speaking). It's how we learn language as a child; first we listen and then eventually we speak. As we get older, we first learn to read and then we write.

Therefore if your students are at an extremely low level, it can sometimes be unrealistic to focus extensively on speaking if they don't have a solid grasp of reading or listening skills. Even though the class is a "conversation" class, you can slip in some work on these other skills each class and this will really help your students get ready to speak later.

In fact, most of the textbooks in use today introduce the target grammar or vocabulary through a reading or listening exercise. Since it's a "conversation" class, it can be tempting to skip over this and get straight to the speaking part of the lesson but keep in mind that these things are actually quite useful for our lower level students for building a solid foundation.

All four skills are intricately connected and can be hard to separate but it isn't really necessary to do this. The best classes are often those that delicately balance these four skills and so even in "conversation" or "speaking" classes, don't be afraid to include some of the other three skills as well, although your class should be heavier on the speaking if that is what the students and administration at your school expect of you. Don't forget to think beyond your class and see language learning as a holistic process that happens over years and decades.

In addition, you could also focus on some functional speaking skills, which in some ways are easier to teach and learn than just general speaking because they are so specific and the language is often quite controlled with a very limited range of variations. For example, you could work on giving advice with beginners by teaching them how to use *maybe you could/should* (very polite), *should/shouldn't* (more polite) and *you'd better/you'd better not* (less polite). The level of politeness would depend on the context you've chosen to introduce the language.

Another function to teach beginners is apologizing. Something like, "I'm (really) sorry, I _____" is very useful and doesn't require complicated grammar or vocabulary.

Finally, agreeing and disagreeing are also useful and they don't involve complicated grammar. Things like: Really? Me too. I think so too. Ummm how about _____?, are within the grasp of most beginners.

Focus on Vocabulary

One of the main reasons that students cannot converse freely is that they lack the vocabulary to be able to do so. In my experience, this is a far bigger problem for absolute beginners than lack of grammatical knowledge. Think about your own experiences in learning a language—I'm sure you knew what you wanted to say and perhaps even knew the grammar construction that you needed to use but probably just couldn't access that elusive, but necessary word.

Spend some time each class teaching a few new words to your students (5-10 is ideal) and it will be time well spent. However, be careful not to overwhelm students with too many because then they may not actually remember anything! I find that the ideal amount is five new words per class, which is an amount that anyone can remember quite easily and it's also often possible to maintain these until the next class. Of course, you should review words periodically as well so that they remain in the student's working memory and are more readily accessible to them when needed.

Build Confidence

If your students are high school students or adults and have been studying English for years but are still extremely low level, it's highly likely that they have little to no confidence in their English abilities. Remember to meet students where they're at and don't praise only the top students in the class, but also praise the lower level ones too for any small improvement that they make. Even a simple thing like having a positive attitude towards English that day in class or participating sincerely in a game or activity can be praised. Remember that even a small comment can go a long way towards building confidence and increasing motivation.

Consider Doing Some Presentations in Speaking or Conversation Classes

There are a number of reasons why you might consider using presentations in classes.

#1: Presenting is a Tangible Skill

Although I'm here to teach English, I always try to give my students some tangible skills they can take with them into the real world. For example, in a writing class, I teach students about hooks, thesis statements and topic sentences. This will be useful in any kind of writing, in any kind of language.

In my conversational English classes, I like to teach some presentation skills like eye contact, gestures, etc. Hopefully they'll use these things again in the future.

#2: They're Ideal for Business Students

Many business people have to do presentations at work. Help students get some practice with this important skill in your classes.

#3: They Help to Improve Listening Skills

When else do students listen for an hour or two, in English that's almost exactly at their level? During presentations. Just be sure to give some task to give students a reason to listen.

#4: Presentations are Student Directed

I generally give some very vague guidelines as far as topics go. For example, any current events topic. Or, food/school/culture/history/hobbies. Not just one of these things, but perhaps all of them!

This way, students are free to choose whatever they're interested in and care about. They are often more willing to learn new vocabulary than if I were to just assign a random topic. Of course, for best results, do be strict about time limits, PowerPoint slides, etc.

#5: Presentations are a Break from the Usual

Teacher talks, students listen. Sounds familiar? Mix it up in your classes, and have the students do all the talking that day. It's good for them and good for you too!

Tips for Making a More Student-Centered Classroom

These days, all the current language acquisition research advocates student-centered classrooms. This is for good reason! Teacher-centered classrooms, beyond the very basic level of learning a language, or for extremely young learners have largely proven to be ineffective at creating students who can actually communicate in a meaningful way. Sure, you can possibly cram grammar and vocabulary into students but in terms of them taking this knowledge and using it in a real-way, teacher-centered classrooms just don't work.

Of course, it's sometimes not easy when all the students speak the same language, but it is indeed possible.

Teacher Centered Classrooms: One Disturbing Example

I remember one time that I was teaching across the hall from one of my colleagues and could overhear his class and how it was teacher-centered to the extreme. To the extreme! I can't really emphasize this enough. Like this person basically was "on-stage" shouting out vocabulary words for 20 minutes out of the 50 minute class. There were only one second breaks in between the words, so maybe the students were repeating them? I have no idea because I couldn't actually hear the students, at all.

The teacher would have done well to heed these tips!

#1: Groups

It's all about partners or groups of 3, 4, or 5. Beyond that maximum number is often too big to be effective because not everyone will be able to participate. I like to make groups randomly instead of allowing the students to choose because it keeps them on their toes, you know?

And don't even think about having a prolonged class discussion if you have more than 8 or 10 student in your class. There just isn't enough student talking time in this scenario. Students often want this, but don't give it to them because in the end, it's not what they really need.

#2: Set-up an activity (give them a task) and step back

Supervise and give gentle correction or feedback, but don't interfere if the group is doing a good job on their task. If they're heading down the wrong path, use a firmer hand but once you do this, step away again and give them a chance to do it on their own.

#3: Lecture, if you must, but only in 3-5 minute intervals

Students will often not pay attention for anything beyond a few minutes of lecturing, especially in a second language. I prefer not to lecture at all but will often give students a worksheet of some kind to get them to discover the target grammar or vocabulary on their own. After the lecture or guided discovery, use some activities to get students to practice what they're just heard or figured out.

And, if you must do the lecture thing be sure to use some visuals like a simple PowerPoint presentation or some short video clips to illustrate your point. Anything to break up the endless teacher talking thing!

Consider Using this Speaking Rubric for Tests

Here are some of the most important factors to keep in mind when evaluating speaking for your English learners. This rubric works well with elementary school students to college students or adults. And it's quite a helpful framework for cutting through all the confusion and being able to simply separate the top students from the weaker ones. You can also get away from looking simply for errors into rewarding students who go above and beyond that.

There are also a million and one ways to evaluate speaking tests with an English speaking rubric. However, I always prefer the simple way for just about anything, especially with language learners.

If you look on the Internet, you'll notice that lots of other people have talked about this before. But, a lot of the other ESL speaking rubrics you see are so complicated that I don't think their students will actually understand them.

I'd rather make it simple and easy to understand for my students. I want them to know how to get a good score on the test when they're studying for it. It just seems fair. I have three categories in my speaking rubric, and each one is worth an equal number of points.

ESL Speaking Rubric: 3 Sections

Let's get to the three categories in my Speaking Rubric.

Grammar and vocabulary (10 points)

Interesting, detailed answers (10 points)

Good questions (10 points)

This rubric is not just useful for English tests, but could be applied to any foreign language.

#1: Grammar and Vocabulary

This section does not cover all vocabulary and grammar possible in the English language but only what we studied in class up to that point. For example, if I'd been teaching passive forms, I'd expect students to use that when appropriate for the topic.

Including ALL English grammar and vocabulary isn't really fair, especially for beginner level students.

If I've been teaching about laws and punishment, I'd expect students to use vocabulary terms like jaywalking, shoplifting, life sentence and parole in their answer, if appropriate. Simple words or talking around these words by describing them but not actually saying them would result in a deduction.

For example, using "walking across the street not at the correct place" would be considered incorrect if I've clearly taught "jaywalking" in class. Students know to expect this so it's not a surprise to them! I give numerous examples related to this when explaining the test in class.

I also include other very simple, basic things that students at their level would be expected to have down cold. For example, high-intermediate students should have a very firm grasp on using the simple past and not make mistakes, even though we may not have explicitly studied it.

Absolute beginners require special consideration for this because they usually have no English skills beyond what you've taught them. In this case, I stick almost exclusively to what they've learned in my class.

#2: Interesting, Detailed Answers

This means that students should not just give very simple answers to their partner but should elaborate with one or two extra details. I encourage this is in class every single day so a failure to do this on the test does not make me happy!

Have the students actually thought about the topics and subjects discussed and aren't just giving answers straight out of the textbook? Yes? Great. No, you won't score that highly on this section.

Basically, is it easy to have a conversation with this student or not. The best students will find it very easy to get a perfect score in this section.

1 Example

For example, if a student asks the question:

Q: What do you think is a big problem facing students in Korea these days?

A: Maybe cell-phone addiction.

This answer would result in a very low score. They should have elaborated with 1-2 supporting details. Or, even a follow-up question to their partner would have been okay. As it is, the burden is on their partner to keep the conversation going.

That said, I always tell students that 1-2 details is enough. Nobody likes having a conversation with someone who won't stop talking!

#3: Interesting Questions

This involves actually listening to their partner and asking appropriate follow-up questions in order to keep the conversation going.

It also involves thinking of an interesting way to start the conversation, since I just give my students very general topics but leave the actual conversation starter up to them. Since I give my students the topics a couple of weeks before the test, there's almost no excuse except laziness to not have an interesting conversation starter!

I always give plenty of ridiculous examples when I'm explaining the test about all kinds of terrible follow-up questions. It's funny but it seems to work and most students do quite well in this section. Students are free to ask any sort of question they want to follow-up on something but it has to match the answer that they heard.

1 Example

Q: What's a big problem facing students in Korea these days?

A: I think student debt. Lots of families can't afford to pay for university anymore, so students have to take on debt. But, it's a big burden when they graduate because they can't save money for a house.

Q: So, what about cell-phone addiction?

This is a terrible follow-up question. The second student gave quite an interesting answer, but the first student didn't even listen to it. The follow-up question should have been related to student debt.

What Does your Evaluation Paper Look Like?

The paper that I use to log scores on is super simple.

Name:

ID#:

Grammar + vocabulary 1 2 3 4 5

Interested, detailed answers 1 2 3 4 5

Good questions 1 2 3 4 5

Comments:

Tips for Teaching Listening

Students have Different Needs in Terms of Listening

This may be obvious to some teachers so please forgive me if this is the case for you. However, with regards to listening, students have very different needs. Some of them may include the following:

- Preparing for an English proficiency exam like IELTS, TOEIC, or TOEFL

- Traveling and having to navigate airports, immigration counters or haggling at a market

- Wanting to watch English TV shows and movies without subtitles

- Those preparing to study abroad in an English speaking country

- People who have to do an English interview for some kind of job

These are only just a few examples. If you're not sure why your students want to improve their listening skills—ask them. Then, you'll be able to tailor your listening lesson to that. Someone wanting to improve their listening skills for travel has very different needs from someone hoping for a certain score on the TOEIC listening test. They both have differing needs from someone hoping to be able to understand a university physics lecture in English!

Figure out the Technology Before Class Starts

Get familiar with the technology you'll be using during class, before class. Nothing is worse than a teacher trying to figure out how to play the audio during class time as it looks very unprofessional. If you have access to the classroom you'll be teaching in, go test the equipment with the recordings/files you'll be using, and make sure that the tech works with the audio files/CD as well as that you know how to use the equipment. Waiting until a few minutes before class may not give you enough time to call the school computer tech (who may not be available, and you may not have the phone number for), and other obstacles may arise that you don't have time to manage or problem solve. Computers randomly update and remotes can go missing.

Also don't forget to check the audio level. Sometimes it can be a little bit difficult to hear it from the back of the class. Even if you ask your students, "Can you hear it?," some of them will say yes even if they can't if they're a little bit shy. The only way to know for sure is to stand at the back of the class and see for yourself!

How Many Times Should I Play the Listening Passage?

Playing the listening passage twice is ideal. If the students understand everything on the first run-through, it's probably too easy. If they struggle to understand the main ideas even on the second time through, it's too difficult. This is a good general rule of thumb you can use for your listening lessons but feel free to adapt it as necessary.

Sometimes it may be necessary to read the script yourself at a slower speed, and with pauses between phrases of sentences, or after a difficult sentence or section of the text before continuing to speak the next part.

Consider Some Listening Focused Lessons in Conversation Classes

You can plan a whole class around a listening passage. It's nice to mix things up a bit and give students a break from classes heavy on speaking and conversation.

Why consider doing this? There are a few important reasons. First of all, you will most certainly have introverted students in your classes who appreciate some quieter activities. Secondly, listening is a very important skill and one that certainly requires some dedicated practice time.

Furthermore, they can give students a chance to practice the micro-skills used when listening to passages on the TOEIC/TOEFL exams. Or, give students some confidence and practice with real-life situations when traveling.

Listening Passages: Check the Textbook First

If you use a textbook, it's usually a gold mine in terms of listening passages and using it can save a ton of time searching around on the Internet for something that'll work. Make use of them because they'll often be at the perfect level of your students. In addition, they'll usually recycle the grammar and vocabulary from earlier chapters which can be a nice source of review for our students.

Beyond that, there are some other go-to sources for listening passages that I like to use. Check at the end of this book for a more detailed list filled with recommendations.

Listening Exercises: Ideal for Homework Assignments

Consider listening activities for homework. Perhaps something like watching a certain *YouTube* video and writing (or speaking) a quick response to it might be one that you consider. Or, if the listening passages in your textbook are easily available online, then consider assigning them, along with some questions for homework assignments.

You could also consider giving students a few questions that are the same type and style as are found on the TOEIC/TOEFL exams. Or, real-life comprehension tasks such as figuring out when a train leaves for a specific destination but the speaker is saying several departure times together.

Listen for One Specific Thing

Maybe you've had this experience when studying another language? It's really easy to feel overwhelmed when listening to something a little bit difficult. The words are washing over you, but you're not really taking anything in besides a few random words. You probably felt extremely frustrated.

I think this can often be how our students feel, especially if their listening skills are a little bit weaker than their classmates. One thing that we can do to help them out is by giving them one specific thing to listen for. Ask students if they know and use the reading skill scanning for specific information in a reading passage. Ask them if they're good at doing it— and then point out that the same scanning skill is used in listening. It can be a certain vocabulary item, grammatical point, or some answers to very basic true/false questions. These are just a few quick examples. The key is to tell students what you want them to listen for before hitting "play."

It's Not Just about Native Speakers from North America

According to one estimate, there are 380 million native English speakers and more than *700 million* non-native speakers. What does this mean for our students? They are twice as likely to encounter a non-native speaker than a native one.

As teachers, we can help our students out with different English accents and use some listening passages with people from around the world. Most ESL/EFL textbooks are quite good at this these days but if the specific book you're using isn't, it's easy to find a huge variety of English speakers on *Youtube*.

Give Students a Reason to Listen

The key to better results when teaching listening is to give students a reason to listen beyond just, "listen to this!" How do you that? By having some tasks that students need to complete. It could be as simple as answering some true/false questions or some more detailed comprehension questions.

Perhaps they need to listen carefully to what another student is saying in order to ask an appropriate follow-up question. Or, maybe they have to listen to an answer provided by another student in order to make a judgement about whether it's correct or incorrect. Maybe they have to listen to what the teacher is saying in order to dictate it correctly onto their paper. Whatever the case, there should always be a reason for listening.

Don't Forget About Two-Way Communication!

Remember that listening is more than students just listening to the teacher talk. Or, students listening to a passage or conversation of some kind on *YouTube* or from the textbook. A valuable source of listening practice is students talking to each other. It's actually my preferred form of listening practice because it's two-way communication and it gives students a chance to respond to what they heard.

Get Familiar with Listening Sub-Skills

When planning a listening lesson, it can be immensely helpful to always have the following list of sub-skills in the back of your mind. Then, for each activity that you do, think about which sub-skill it's working on.

Prediction

If you are watching TV and see a woman in formal business attire with pictures of sun, clouds and thunder, then you're going to expect to hear a weather forecast. Or, you'd expect to hear certain words, phrases or topics during a university lecture and other ones while listening to little children playing together. Finally, there are some standard phrases you'd expect to hear at the supermarket or when ordering a drink at a coffee shop.

Why is prediction useful in listening? It primes our brains to understand what we're listening to. We can help our students out with this skill by giving them a little bit of information about what they're going to hear, perhaps a title or picture and then asking them to predict what the people might say. Or, some of the vocabulary that they could expect to hear in a certain context.

Listening for Gist

Unless you're almost fluent, when listening to something in another language, chances are that you might not pick up every single word that's being said. When reading, it's easy enough to stop, analyze the grammar or get a dictionary out to look up unknown words. However, listening usually happens in real time and this isn't always possible.

One way that we can help our students out with this is to get them to focus on the most important words (nouns, adjectives and verbs) that can give the bigger picture of something. This is called listening for gist.

Something we can do to help our students is find a short video clip. Then, get students to predict what it might be about based on the title. Play the clip and ask students to pick out 5-10 of the most important words.

Listening for Transition Signals or Discourse Markers

When driving, traffic lights and signs help us understand what's coming up ahead. There are also similar things in language, especially in more formal situations like presentations or lectures. For example, during a presentation someone might say something like, "I'm going to talk about three important reasons. First . . ., next . . ., finally . . ." The first, next and finally indicate that the speaker is moving on to the next part of their talk.

One way to help our students with this is to find a business presentation or a short lecture. Then, get students to listen and try to identify these transition signals.

Listening for Detail or Specific Information

Sometimes it's necessary to listen for a specific detail such as a number, name, object, time, etc. When doing this, it's usually okay to ignore things that don't seem relevant, essentially filtering the information.

A way to help our students practice this is to give them some specific questions before listening. They can be simple true/false questions that can be answered upon the first listening. Or, more detailed comprehension questions that would require a second time listening.

Inferring Meaning

In some situations, even if we don't understand exactly what was said, it's possible to infer the meaning. For example, in a loud bar or restaurant if you hand a credit card to the waiter, they may mumble something and have an apologetic look on their face. Even if you didn't understand exactly what they said, you'd probably infer that they didn't take credit cards or that their machine is broken and you may need to use cash.

Or, if we hear a conversation about homework and then some sort of excuse as to why it isn't done, we could easily infer that the conversation is between a student and a teacher. This is done through the use of contextual clues.

A way to help our students with this is to find a short video clip from a TV show or movie on *YouTube*. Play the dialogue but don't show the video. Then, students have to infer what is taking place, who is talking, where they are, etc. Show the original clip with video this time and students can see if their inferences were correct.

Note Taking

An important listening skill for some students is note taking. This is especially true if they plan to study in an English speaking country, particularly at the university level where lectures are commonly the main method of giving information. Related closely to this is the need to distinguish the main ideas from the supporting ones in order to keep up!

There are a number of activities we can do to help our students with this, including having students identify the most important words from a listening passage or video. Or, just writing down 1-2 words of their partner's response to a question and not the entire answer word for word.

Listening for Attitude, Feeling or Mood

Knowing and recognizing the mood of the speaker often makes it easier to predict the content. For example, if someone is angry or upset at a store or restaurant, we can expect to hear some complaint about the food or service. Or, if someone is happy at a sporting even, we can predict that their team is doing well and we can expect to hear different things than if their team was losing.

Use this ESL Listening Lesson Plan Template

If you want to plan a listening focused lesson, there are a few basics steps you can follow. This template loosely follows the framework as set forth in the CELTA teacher training course.

Set the Context

This introduces the theme of your listening topic. For example, if your listening is about shopping, you could ask students whether or not they ever buy things without trying them on and whether or not they've had good or bad experiences with that.

Or, if your topic is travel, you could ask students what are things that people do while they're spending time waiting at an airport. It's best to have students discuss the question for a couple minutes with their partner and then quickly elicit some answers from the class.

Pre-Listening Task

Next, you'll need to assign students a pre-listening task. Some of my favorites are prediction tasks which lead into the next step. For example, if the topic is problems while traveling, students can think of five common travel problems with a partner. Elicit answers and write some of them on the board.

You could also show students a picture and have them predict something based on that. Or, you could introduce some of the vocabulary words from the listening that you think the students won't know.

Listening, Round #1

The students listen for the main idea of the passage the first time. You can have them see if their prediction were true, if you did this in step #2. Or, you could give them some very simple T/F questions. They could listen for something related to sequence and order. Finally, you may want to have students listen for some specific words, expressions or grammatical construction. Basically, anything that gives them a reason to listen but it should NOT be listening for the finer details (this is the next step).

Have students compare answers with a partner and then quickly go over them together with the class, but don't spend too much time with this. You don't want to give away too many details because they'll listen one more time in the next step.

Listening, Round #2

Give students some more difficult comprehension questions, they'll listen again, check answers with a partner and then with the class. You can spend a bit more time discussing the answers if necessary than you would in the previous step.

Or, if you're using a listening passage to introduce a grammar concept, students could listen for that specific item. For example, subject and object pronouns. And then answer some questions about who each pronoun refers back to.

Pronunciation (optional)

If there are some words that are difficult to pronounce or your students particularly struggle with this, then you may want to focus a little bit on pronunciation.

Do some drills and practice using the words from the listening passage.

Application

Students have to apply the concepts from the listening to their own lives in order to make it more memorable. The best kind of activities are ones that involve students giving their opinions, such as asking them if they agree or disagree with a certain thing related to the listening passage.

Or, you could have students do a survey and discuss the answers. Another idea is to have them pretend to be one of the people in the listening while the other one is a news reporter and they interview each other. Get creative and make listening fun and interesting! The activities and games in this book are an excellent starting place.

Follow Up

After finishing this, the sky is the limit in terms of what you can do. You might consider switching over to focus on other skills such as speaking or writing. Or, you could have students do a presentation related to the listening passage. Maybe you can play a game of some kind with them. Get creative in terms of how you tie what you do next to what the students have listened to. I generally try to stick with a unified theme throughout the entire class though.

Tips for Finding Listening Passages

If you want to know where you can find ESL listening exercises, here are a few of my go-to sources.

The Textbook

All ESL textbooks these days have listening exercises in them. They are often the best source for listening passages because they'll be related to the grammar and vocabulary that the students are learning. Plus, in theory, they should be at the perfect level and recycle vocabulary from previous lessons which is a nice way for our students to get some review in.

Breaking News English

Apart from the textbook, *Breaking News English* (www.breakingnewsenglish.com) is my go-to source for listening passages. It's got a huge variety of current events and best of all, the passages are graded and divided into various levels, complete with exercises. This makes it super easy to use them. Plus, the topics lend themselves well to great discussions.

Business English Pod

If you teach Business English, *Business English Pod* (www.businessenglishpod.com) is pure gold. There is a paid version, but I've found the free version has enough of what I need to make it work. Their listening passages are excellent and are a nice starting point for further work.

YouTube and *English Central*

Of course, *YouTube* is a gold mine for all things listening. They have millions of videos. But, how to find the right one for your students? I usually just search for the topic + ESL. For example, "jobs + ESL," or, "sports + ESL" and have found what I was looking for in a minute or two.

For more advanced level students, consider using authentic material from *YouTube*. By that, I mean materials that aren't specifically designed for ESL students.

You may also want to consider using *English Central* which is kind of like *YouTube* but for English learners.

Podcasts

The best thing about podcasts is that it's super easy to listen to them on the go so you may want to consider assigning them to your students for listening homework. Plus, there's a podcast for any level or topic of interest, including some specific ones for English learners.

Another great thing is that most podcast players have a setting that makes it easy to reduce the speed. I find that 3/4 speed works well for most English learners. Your students may be tempted to go to 1/2 speed but this is usually too slow and the pronunciation can sound really strange, unless the person speaks extremely quickly.

Here are some of my podcast recommendations for English learners (you can find most of them wherever you normally find podcasts, or at the website listed):

- *Serial:* www.serialpodcast.org (advanced)

- *Business English Pod*: www.businessenglishpod.com (intermediate-advanced)

- *The British Council*: www.learnenglish.britishcouncil.org (beginner-advanced)

- *Podcasts in English*: www.podcastsinenglish.com (beginner-advanced)

- *This American Life:* www.thisamericanlife.org (intermediate-advanced)

- *Radiolab:* www.wnycstudios.org/podcasts/radiolab (intermediate-advanced)

- *Slow English*: www.slowenglish.info (beginner)

TV and Movies

When students ask me about how to improve their listening skills, I often recommend that they watch some English TV shows or movies. They're a nice way to get some serious extensive listening in.

However, when choosing a TV show or film, there are several points to consider and this is the advice that I give my students.

- Is it interesting? There are lists of "Best Movies to Learn English" all over the Internet, but if the films are in genres you don't like, you are less likely to get much out of it.

- Is it something you could watch over and over? Unless your English is advanced, you will learn more each time you watch the same show. So, pick something you will enjoy re-watching as much as you enjoyed watching for the first time.

- Think about accents. Some accents are easier to understand than others. For example, Tom Hanks speaks slowly and clearly, but Sylvester Stallone sounds tired or a little drunk and is more difficult to understand.

- Consider the genre. Action movies will be easier to understand because there are visual cues (the action) to assist with understanding. Dramas and romantic comedies will have more "sitting and talking" scenes and more difficult language.

- Consider the level of the English. It's ideal if you can understand at least 50% of what the people are saying without too much effort. 70 or 80% is even better.

- Subtitles: Try without! Using subtitles can make it far too easy and it's often not a great way to improve listening skills.

Of course, a teacher can also use clips from TV shows or movies, or an entire episode or movie in your classes too. Just be sure to assign some pre-listening activities, things that students have to listen for during the clip and then some post-listening activities too. This will help our students get the most value out of this listening activity.

Tips for Teaching Writing

Student-Centred Teaching is ALWAYS Best

When teaching a language, whether speaking, writing, listening or reading, student-centred is always the way to go. What I mean by this is that students should be doing the work, not you! What exactly does this mean when teaching writing?

Students Improve by Spending More Time Writing and Reading

The best way to improve writing is to write and edit lots and also examine good examples of English writing! Design your classes so that students are getting as much practice as possible.

Freedom for What to Write About

Whenever possible, students should have some degree of freedom to choose what they want to write about. For example, they can choose from among five different essay topics. Or, they are free to write an opinion essay about any topic as long as they check in with me first to make sure it's suitable.

Responsibility for Final Product is With the Students

Most importantly, you'll certainly want to avoid the trap of, "Teacher is responsible for correcting all errors in my writing." This is especially true if you want to have a life outside of teaching. Furthermore, it's best to equip students to go out into the real world where bosses aren't standing over their shoulder every time they have to send an important email to a client in English.

The Better Way: Self-Editing

The teacher being responsible for the final product is not ideal. What's the better way? Teaching self-editing. After all, isn't that what happens when your students have to write something at work? Or, take an English proficiency exam? It's certainly the better way so keep this in the back of your mind when designing your lessons and assigning homework.

Use a Grading Rubric for Evaluating Writing

For English teachers, grading writing and speaking are not easy when compared to things like grammar or vocabulary because there's often no right or wrong answer. Everything falls on a continuum from needs improvement to excellent.

The challenge for teachers is to grade in a way that's fair and that also appears this way to the students. To do this, you'll need an ESL writing rubric. I generally use the same one with all my writing classes and for a wide variety of topics. Of course, feel free to adapt it to suit your needs for each situation.

This rubric started off more complicated but over the years I've simplified it. The best rubrics are simple enough that students can clearly understand why they received the grade that they did.

The Categories I Evaluate for English Writing

Each of these five categories has an equal number of possible points (from 0-5), for a total of 25 points. To make grading easier, if the essay is worth 30%, adjust the rubric to make each category out of six points. Or for 20%, make it out of four points.

If you make each section out of four points, you can use something like the following:

1 = inadequate

2 = needs improvement

3 = meets expectations

4 = exceeds expectations

Here are the categories that I look at when evaluating writing.

1. sentences/paragraphs/format

2. grammar/spelling/punctuation/vocabulary

3. hook/thesis statement/topic sentences/ideas

4. task completion/effect on the reader

#1: Sentence Structure, Paragraphs, and Format

The best essays have sentences and paragraphs that are complete and easy to read. A nice variety of conjunctions and transitions are used to join them together.

#2: Grammar, Spelling, Punctuation, and Vocabulary

The best pieces of writing may only have 1-2 small errors in this area. There is a good use of higher level grammar and vocabulary.

This section includes pretty much all the formatting, language (vocabulary and grammar) that a student at their level would be expected to know, even if we explicitly haven't discussed it in class.

I will give my students a heads up about what I'm looking for. For example, if the essay topic lends itself to using the simple past and the students are intermediate or advanced, I'll mention that I expect their verbs to be perfect. I haven't explicitly taught this grammar point in my writing class but it's something that students at this level should know cold, especially when writing because they have time to think about it and look it up if necessary.

Or the writing piece may lend itself to lots of descriptive words (adjectives and adverbs). I'll mention to my higher-level students that I expect to see some interesting ones that are not the following: good, better, best, bad, beautiful, fun, nice, funny, slowly, quickly, etc. Which ones they specifically use are up to them but my hope is that students push themselves a little bit with this and produce a piece of writing that is rich and alive.

#3: Hook, Thesis Statement, and Topic Sentence

To get full marks, all of these will have to be very well done. This is because I teach these things extensively in class and ensure that if students take away one thing from my writing course, it's how to do these things.

For certain kinds of writing, these components may not be found. However, there are other key pieces that will be needed to give structure and organization to the writing piece. I change this section to fit the writing style as needed.

#4: Ideas

The ideas in the writing are clear, logical, and well organized. Good supporting facts and information are used. If it's a take-home assignment, I expect it to include real statistics and facts because students can look them up on the Internet. If the essay is for a test written in class, then good logic will have to be used.

#5: Task Completion and Effect on the Reader

The best essays are easy to understand on a first, quick read-through. The student also followed the directions for the assignment (word count, etc.).

Show Students the Rubric When Explaining the Assignment

Something I try to be 100% clear about with my students whether it's a written assignment or a speaking test is how I'm going to evaluate it. In this case, when I'm explaining the assignment, I give students this rubric and go through it section by section to explain what I'm looking for. Students appreciate knowing what the expectations are and it'll save you a lot of time too because students will mostly understand why they got the grade that they did.

Can I Evaluate ESL/EFL Writing Without a Rubric?

You may be tempted to evaluate student writing without a rubric because you think it will save time. I don't recommend this unless you're teaching informally and the grades and feedback you give students don't count towards an official grade of some kind.

However, when teaching at a university in a credit class, grades matter and teachers need to have a reason for why they assigned the grade they did. Beyond that simple fact, here's why teachers should use a rubric to evaluate written work.

Writing rubrics help teachers and students in many ways. They save teachers huge amounts of time because students understand exactly how they got their grades. You will avoid a steady stream of students wanting to come to office hours and demand every deducted point be explained. A rubric helps students process the feedback and have a better idea about what specific writing skills need to improve. Lastly, if a student goes to your school admin and demands their grade be raised, it's easier for the teacher to show how and why a student got their grade. When I taught in Korean universities, there were a number of times when students challenged their scores or grades.

Giving Feedback when Teaching Writing

When I teach English writing to intermediate or advanced level students, I'm ALL about teaching self-editing instead of having students rely on me to correct their errors. However, during the semester, students are free to come to my office during my allotted hours to have a quick read-through of their writing. I'll usually give feedback along the lines of:

"Your thesis statement is kind of weak. Have a look at that and see if you can make it more concise."

"I noticed that you have very few transitions in your essay. It makes it kind of hard to read. Try adding in at least five of them"

"You have many grammar errors. For example, subject-verb agreement."

"Can you try to use some more complicated grammar or vocabulary? It's fine, but all the sentences are so similar and also quite simple."

"Pay closer attention to punctuation. For example, _____."

Beginners will require more personalized feedback from the teacher because they are usually not at the level where they are able to identify their own errors.

What about Feedback on Assignments and Tests?

Along with my grading rubric, I'll write some comments on my students' work, usually 3-4 sentences next to their grade. Throughout their essay, I'll also pick out around five things to circle as problems or errors.

I'll put a check mark as a sign of a good thing like the thesis statement or topic sentences.

Is it necessary to correct every single error? Not really. It's often more helpful to just point out mistakes that students have made more than once. That way, they have something solid to improve upon instead of just a whole bunch of seemingly unrelated mistakes.

Which ESL Writing Textbook Do you Recommend?

Are you looking for an excellent textbook for teaching academic writing to ESL or EFL students? Stop looking right now and go buy this: *Great Writing 4: From Great Paragraphs to Great Essays* by Keith Folse. You can easily find it on *Amazon*. Actually, this whole series is excellent from the first book to the last and you really don't need to consider any other!

The fourth book is an ideal introduction to writing an essay for high intermediate to advanced level English students. In my case, I used it when teaching 3rd or 4th year English majors at a university in South Korea.

How Do I Prevent Cheating in a Writing Class?

If you teach writing in a for-credit class where you have to assign grades, you will almost certainly have students who try to cheat. There are a few things that I do to combat this and make things fair for the students.

Homework Assignments are Not Worth that Many Marks

During my writing courses, I do give homework assignments. They just aren't worth that many points. For example, the maximum is 20% of the final grade (usually four assignments worth 5% each).

The bulk of the grade is things we do in class: journaling and then the midterm and final exams that have to be physically written in my classroom. This gives me a better indication of who can write well without having an Internet crutch to assist them.

The Ultimate Thing to Do on the First Day of Writing Class

On the first day of any writing class, I get students to complete a "Get to know you assignment." I give them about 20 minutes to write three short paragraphs that include the following:

- the past (high school days, growing up, etc.)
- the present (university life and their thoughts about it)
- the future (dreams, hopes, etc.)

This shows how proficient students are at the past/present/future verb tenses and it's often quite obvious who will do well in your class and who will likely struggle.

Then, keep these papers and in case of a questionable homework assignment, you have something to compare it to. For example, I had one student submit something that I myself probably couldn't have produced. It was that good and had advanced level vocabulary that I had to look up to find out the meanings to. Plus, there wasn't a single grammatical error in the whole assignment, which is certainly quite unusual for someone who doesn't speak English as their first language. It's even unusual for someone who does!

I pulled out her assignment from the first day and found it riddled with simple mistakes like not using the correct past tense verb form and other similar mistakes. She clearly could not have done that homework assignment herself and my guess is that she paid someone to do it because I was unable to find it through a Google search.

Of course, for some other students I'm able to find their work using Google which makes it easier to deal with.

Midterm/Final Exam: Assign Random Topics

Some teachers assign a single topic for their exams and then allow the students to prepare their essay beforehand. During the exam, they just have to write it out. I try to avoid this.

Instead, I give students a list of around 20 possible topics. Then, I give students a slip of paper with two possible choices that they must choose from. Each student gets a random combination or two choices so there is no chance to copy off a neighbor.

This allows students to prepare for the exam in terms of ideas and main points, but they can't memorize an essay word for word. I find it to be a better test of writing ability and there's clearly no way to cheat on this kind of exam.

How Can I Foster Student Autonomy in Writing Classes?

Autonomy, with regards to teaching, is when students take charge of their own learning. That is, they are responsible for it and the teacher is more of a guide than the all-knowing one who imparts wisdom and knowledge.

Teacher as Editor Model: Bad News!

I believe that the current model of teaching writing in most universities in Korea (and perhaps around the world where English is taught as a second or foreign language) does nothing to foster student autonomy. When I attend conferences, I hear people giving presentations about teaching writing without even a mention of self-editing, instead focusing on teacher, or peer-editing, exclusively.

This model of teacher editor is basically where the student writes something and gives it to the teacher, probably with very little in the way of self-editing, if any at all.

In fact, it's not so uncommon that the student (especially at lower-levels) will give something to the teacher that came straight from Google Translate. Then the teacher spends ridiculous amounts of time editing something that in some cases is barely understandable and gives it back to the student. They make the necessary changes, often mindlessly and don't really look at the mistakes in detail. And then hand it in to the teacher again.

This cycle can repeat endlessly without the student improving their writing!

Peer as Editor: Bad News Also!

This same cycle can also be done with peer editing, which I am not a big fan of either. In both of these models, the learner essentially takes very little responsibility for turning out a quality product on their own because they know that the teacher or friend will just make the changes they need.

However, peer or teacher editing is 100% unlike real life. When students are taking an English proficiency test that involves writing, there is no teacher or friend sitting next to them, helping them along. Nor would they have this at any job. They would just be expected to turn out a decent email or essay or whatever else they would need to write by themselves.

How about Teaching Self-Editing Instead?

In an attempt to foster student autonomy by teaching writing strategies, I teach students to self-edit by giving them check-lists with things like:

1. Check all the verbs: correct tense?

2. What is your thesis statement? Circle it! Is it stated or implied? Underline the topic sentences. Put a box around your restated thesis.

3. Does each sentence have a capital letter and period/question mark/exclamation point? Circle them.

Include Writing in Speaking and Conversation Classes

Just because you teach a conversation class doesn't mean that you shouldn't throw a little bit of writing practice in there too! Why should you consider doing this? Here are a few important reasons.

First of all, some students are introverted. I'm a bit of an introvert myself and nothing makes me more tired than a class full of upbeat and cheery conversation activities. That's why I like to incorporate some quieter, individual work into each lesson. A short writing exercise or activity of some kind based on the topic of the day is ideal for this.

Secondly, nothing solidifies grammar or vocabulary more solidly than writing it down on a piece of paper. I think it's sometimes the case where we teach something and students practice it by speaking, but then it never really gets to the next level of actually "knowing" it. Writing can help our students get there and it also gives you the chance to offer some very specific feedback to every single student, which often isn't the case in bigger speaking classes.

Finally, English writing is an important skill that many students don't feel confident with because they don't practice it enough. At least in South Korea where I taught for many years, it'd be normal for English majors to take 10+ speaking or conversation courses, but only 1-2 writing courses. That's why in those speaking ones, I tried to incorporate a little bit of writing. Think about the big picture for your students and whether or not they need more writing practice. If they do, maybe you can be the one to give it to them!

Teach the Writing Process

Most teachers probably already know this from their university days, but it can be helpful to see it written out! When writing, use the writing process. Students can use this for just about anything.

Step 1: Pre-writing — Think about what you're going to write. Brainstorm some ideas.

Choose the best ideas and make an outline. The outline can be very simple, or very detailed. It depends on you. However, don't write full sentence in the outline. Only make a few notes.

Step 2: Writing — Take your ideas and make them into sentences and paragraphs. Don't worry about if it's good or not. Your first draft will almost always be terrible!

Step 3: Editing — Read what you've written slowly and carefully. Does it make sense? Are there any errors. You can repeat steps two and three as often as necessary.

Step 4: Formatting the Final Product — This step involves getting it ready for whatever you're using it for. It may be handing it in to a teacher, uploading it on a blog, or entering an essay competition. Whatever the case, there are usually expectations for what the final product should look like.

All About Writing Style

I certainly know that English teachers have differing opinions about academic writing style rules and formats. However, my personal preference is that students write simply and concisely with few errors. I much prefer simple vocabulary and grammatical constructions as opposed to lots of very long sentences with all kinds of conjunctions and clauses.

Why? Think about the reader. There's almost no situation in life that calls for an extremely advanced level writing —except for an academic journal where you'd be judged poorly for communicating your points clearly and easily. No reader should have to go back through your paragraph 2-3 times just to understand the gist of it. Even an academic journal could probably benefit from making its writing more reader-friendly!

Now, consider students who are writing in English (which isn't their first language). This can compound the problem of not getting the point across clearly because there will be grammatical errors and strange vocabulary choices.

If my students can use sentences that are almost perfect, anyone who is reading should be able to understand what they mean quickly and without having to read it again.

What about long, complicated sentences that are filled with errors? It'll likely be far more difficult for the reader to understand the intended meaning, unless the student is quite advanced and able to do this almost perfectly.

Use your own judgement on this, but I will always err on the side of simplicity! Here's the advice that I give my students.

Write Concisely

When writing in some languages such as Korean, the longer the sentences the better! Sentences are very complicated and sometimes even quite difficult for a native speaker to fully understand them. When students try to translate these sentence directly into English, the results are often not good!

Simple English can be beautiful. It doesn't require long, complicated sentences. It's usually better to write concisely and say what you need to in as few words as possible. This is especially true for beginners. It's better to make short, simple, but perfect sentences rather than long, complicated sentences with many grammatical errors. Think simple. Think short. This will help readers be able to understand the writing quickly and easily.

Read Good Quality Models of the Target Writing Style

Reading makes people better writers. If students are preparing for the TOEFL writing section, it's vital that they read high score sample essays. They absorb huge amounts of information while reading these: examples of good hooks, what clearly written topic sentences look like, how paragraphs are structured, how main body paragraphs support a thesis, good thesis statements versus bad ones (show them low score sample essays too), etc.

Perhaps one of the most important writing elements that students learn through reading sample TOEFL essays is exposure to many different thesis statements. This helps them learn how to form an opinion, and also provides a bank of theses that they can draw on when they're in the actual TOEFL exam struggling to form a thesis under time pressure.

Apply this approach to teaching writing, if possible and appropriate, in every writing lesson. Giving students a model reading text that doubles as the model for the writing task and skills they need to learn, practice, and hopefully master is important. If students are learning to write emails, find an online email by a celebrity that is written well, and their motivation to read it closely will be exponentially bigger.

Find a short story written in English by someone from their home country (make sure it has good short story structure and things like paragraphs are well composed), a newspaper editorial on a controversial topic, or take a chapter from a novel that a blockbuster movie is based on, etc. Careful selection of reading samples that are in the genre of writing you teach will facilitate students achieving their writing goals.

Mistakes are Unavoidable

Mistakes are unavoidable. Some students are very hard on themselves when learning to write, especially when it comes to feedback. Here's the advice that I give my students in writing classes.

When learning something new, it's normal to make a lot of mistakes. This is a fact! This applies to anything and not just English! Remember cooking for the first time? It probably wasn't so delicious and took a really long time. The kitchen was likely a disaster too. How about the first time shooting a basketball? It probably didn't go in!

Learning a language is the same. Nobody is good when they start but the key is to keep practicing and getting better. Fear of making mistakes is normal but it's not helpful. The key is to overcome this and just write. Of course, lots of mistakes will happen, however the most important thing is to keep trying.

Have a Positive Attitude about Criticism

The people who are best at English are those that have a positive attitude about criticism. When a teacher or peer gives them feedback about something they wrote, they love it! These people also regularly seek out feedback, and are willing to get it from just about anyone. They realize that they can learn something from a lot of different people. Basically, they want everyone to read their writing and aren't shy about asking!

On the other hand, people who aren't good at English are really shy about sharing their writing with other people. They often feel embarrassed by their lack of writing skill. However, asking for feedback isn't a sign of weakness. Teachers love it when students ask for help! The best students share their writing with lots of people and welcome any ideas that other people have about it.

Don't Forget about Writing Fluency Practice

Most English writing classes and textbooks focus on accuracy. It's much easier for a textbook or teacher to point out grammar and vocabulary errors than to teach how to write quickly. However, it's important to work on both.

The good news is that you can easily do it yourself! Here's how I helped my students with fluency in writing when I taught in South Korean universities.

Get a notebook. Use it only for this, and not for other English writing practice. Each day (or whatever time interval you decide—twice a week, or 10x a month, etc.), give yourself a topic. For example, "My family," or, "Plans for the weekend," or, "Hopes for the future," or, "My favourite book."

Then write about that topic for five minutes (or ten minutes once you get used to it). Put away your cell-phone and dictionary. The goal is to write quickly. Use only grammar and vocabulary that you know. If you don't know how to spell something, just guess. It doesn't matter. Focus on writing quickly!

This is the most important thing—your pen should NEVER stop moving. If you can't think of anything, write this sentence, "I don't know what to write. I don't know what to write. I don't . . ." After two or three times, you'll think of something else! Make sure your pen does not stop moving! Write quickly. Grammar and vocabulary don't matter for this activity.

There certainly is no need to use a cellphone to look up a word you don't know. Just find another word to write, or leave a blank space and you may think of it later. Just keep going.

Over time, you'll notice that the amount you write increases! You can make a simple chart to keep track of this. Count the number of lines you write after each session and mark it on your paper. The quick way to do this is to come up with an average word count per line from the first session and then use that number to count lines during each subsequent session.

Remember that the goal is to write more quickly, not to write accurately. You can work on grammar, vocabulary and structure at other times.

What Can Students Write About?

There are a ton of things students can write about including a short story, picture, life story, hopes for the future and more. Here are more details about each of these things.

A Short Story

For something different, try writing a short fiction story. Think of an idea and start writing! You can write a story for children, teens, or adults. Let your creativity take over. Remember to build some suspense, and of course, include a good hook at the beginning so that people will want to keep reading it.

To make it more interesting, don't use boring words. Check out this handout I give my students filled with descriptive words: www.jackiebolen/words.

A Picture

If you aren't sure what to write about, use a picture. This can be a photo you have taken, one from the Internet or newspaper, or a work of art. You can use it for descriptive writing or as a prompt for creative writing. Here are some questions to get you started:

- What can you see in the picture?

- Are there people? What are they doing? Look at their faces. Happy, sad, angry . . .

- What is the setting? In a house, at a beach, on a city street . . .

- How is the weather?

- What is happening? If you don't know, get creative!

Life Story

It can be good practice to write your life story. This will require you to write using past tense verbs almost entirely. If you need a quick review of past tense verbs, you can check this out (http://www.englishpage.com/verbpage/simplepast.html). For your story, you can start at the very beginning, and go up to the present time, talking about the highlights. Or, you can focus on a specific period in time such as middle school. Another way to write about the past is choose an interesting story, and write specifically about that. Just remember to pay special attention to the verbs!

Hopes for the Future

It can also be good practice to write about the future. This will require you to use future tense verbs. If you're a little unsure about when to use a certain future verb tense, give yourself a quick test (http://www.englishlessonsbrighton.co.uk/future-tenses-exercise/) and see how you do! Once you have the basics of the future tense down, write about your hopes for the future. You can answer the question, "Where do you see yourself in 10 years?"

Forums

No matter what your hobbies or interests are, there are online forums for people with the same interests. Search for some English-language groups focused on topics you are interested in. Simply *Google* (topic)+forum. If the results are in your own language, make sure you are on google.com, rather than your home country. Posts should be related to the group topic, so you are more likely to know or want to know the vocabulary. Posts are also usually quite short, so you won't get overwhelmed by a wall of text. You also shouldn't feel pressure to write a long post.

Facebook Groups

If you would rather use *Facebook* than join another website, don't worry; there are thousands of groups for every interest you can imagine. You may need to change your *Facebook* language to English to get the search results you want. As on forums, *Facebook* posts are usually short, so you won't feel pressure to write a lot. You don't even have to write anything at all until you feel comfortable participating.

Twitter

Twitter is a fun way to practice English writing. Sign-up for a free account and follow some people. Hopefully they will follow you back. You can search for something like, "ESL," or "learn English" to find other English learners like yourself.

Journaling

If you're not in the habit of journaling, it can be a little bit difficult at the beginning. But, start slowly with 4 or 5 sentences per day. You can gradually increase the sentences to 10 or more. Then just keep doing it at least 4 or 5 days a week. Writing every day is best. It gets easier over time and your writing and speaking will both improve.

If you want someone to correct your writing, check out Lang-8. This is a community of native speakers and language learners who correct each other's writing. The catch is, you have to correct someone's writing before you get your writing corrected. The more you help others, the more help you can receive.

Describe a Scene

One problem with practicing writing is that it is often difficult to think of a topic. Many people keep a journal, but if every day you write about the same activities and experiences, you will not improve. This is one idea which will give you endless material to write. Sources of scenes to describe include photos, paintings, TV shows, and movies.

You can simply describe what you see (or picture in your mind, if describing a scene from a book or creating an imaginary scene). To describe a scene from a TV show or movie, imagine you are explaining it to a blind person. If you want more of a challenge, write a story based on a photo or painting. Ask yourself:

Who are the people?
What are they doing?
What emotions are they feeling?
Add sensory details about the sights, sounds, smells, etc. you can see or imagine from the image.

Short Writing Activities for Beginners

Do you want to direct your students to some of the best online resources? Here are some of my favourites.

Get a Pen Pal

If you can coordinate it, pen pals are a very interesting way for students to practice their writing. You can try finding a teacher in another country with similar age students on some of the English teacher *Facebook* groups or forums. Or, your students could find their own pen-pal. More details about this in the next paragraph.

Sites like *Pen Pal World* and *Global Pen Friends* let you search for pen pals all over the world. This is a bit different than the other suggestions because you will just be writing to one another socially. Your pen pal will not be a tutor, study buddy, or language exchange partner. You improve your writing as you communicate with your pen pal who may or may not be a native English speaker. On the other hand, *InterPals* is a site just for language learners looking for language exchange partners. You enter which language you speak and which language you want to study.

You could consider offering this option as a way for students to get bonus points in your class. I've never done it, but have often thought that it'd be a nice option!

Blogging

One way that students can improve their writing and speaking is to start a blog. They can share their ideas, thoughts and daily life with the world. Some of the best free platforms include: *Blogger*, *Tumblr* and *Wordpress*.

Encourage students to share what they post with their friends and family on *Facebook, Twitter, Pinterest* or other social media channels. Encourage the students in the class to comment on each other's blogs with their own thoughts.

Students can also record some short videos and post them on their blog. They'll get better at speaking by practicing speaking, but they'll also get better at writing by preparing an outline (or full script) for their video!

I used to teach university students in South Korea and I assigned videos to my students for homework. Many of the students didn't like it at the time because they were shy. However, at the end of the course, they said it was one of the most useful things they did.

There are various ways that you can get your students blogging. If you have access to a computer lab, you may want to get students doing it during class time. But, set a requirement such as they must complete one blog post with a minimum of 100 words and comment on two other class blogs during that class time. Or, complete it for homework.

Another option is to have students write a certain number of articles as a homework assignment. I've often given my students the option of either journaling in a notebook or doing an online blog. A surprising number chose the blog option!

Tips for Teaching Grammar

Avoid Rocking the Chalk

When I did the CELTA course a few years back, I did what I thought was a very student-centred lesson. After all, the students were talking with each other most of the time, instead of me. I acted as a facilitator more than anything else and I patted myself on the back for a job well done.

Except during the feedback part, my tutor said that my presentation of the language was teacher-centred to the max. I presented all the finer points of the specific English grammar point. I answered questions like a pro. And then I went over the answers to the practice part of the lesson like a champ.

He challenged me to try a self-discovery style of grammar lesson next time. And not to be up at the front of the class talking, with a piece of chalk in my hand for a large amount of the class.

So I did! Instead of lecturing my students on the finer points of English grammar, I made up a worksheet that pointed out the rules with some examples. Students worked through it and then we convened at the end. When they had a few problems, I made note of the important things and the exceptions to the rules they discovered.

The results? It worked well in terms of students grasping the specific grammar point quickly and easily and this is how I've taught most grammar lessons since then. This is especially true for things students have likely seen before. For example, the simple past or "be" verbs.

You could also try the "test-teach-test" approach if students have seen the specific grammatical point before. Basically, you give students a small test before teaching them formally in any way. It can be on a sheet or paper or on the PowerPoint and should take only a few minutes. Then, you look at the answers together and teach students the things that they're a bit shaky on. To finish up, give another test of sorts to see if they've improved. And of course, points out any mistakes they may have made.

Try out some of these ideas for more student-centered teaching for yourself! Remember, the less you're at the front of the classroom talking, the better it is for your student.

Music and Videos: Ideal for Teaching English Grammar

If you want to spice things up a bit in your classes, then consider using some music or videos. For example, I made a lesson based on the Barenaked Ladies song, "If I Had a Million Dollars," to work on conditionals. I've been using it for years now and I would even catch my students singing it to themselves weeks after that class. If that's not some English teaching awesome, I'm not sure what is.

Check out *YouTube* or use some music that you know. *Fluency MC* (https://fluencymc.com/) is a great resource for English rap songs that cover a variety of grammar points. Get creative and remember that teaching English grammar is more than just textbooks and worksheets. There are a million and one fun ways that you can do it.

Here are some of the best song recommendations for a specific grammar objective that you want to cover:

Simple present

"Don't Give Up" – Bruno Mars

"I Say a Little Prayer for You" – Aretha Franklin

Simple past

"The Sound of Silence" – Simon and Garfunkel

"Because You Loved Me" – Celine Dion

"Roar" – Katy Perry

"Seasons in the Sun" – Terry Jacks

Modal verbs

"Haven't Met You Yet" – Michael Buble

"Baby One More Time" – Britney Spears

"Hero" – Enrique Iglesias

Various

"The Best" – Tina Turner (comparatives and superlatives)

"Michael Learns to Rock" – Take Me to Your Heart (adjectives)

"Unbreak My Heart" – Toni Braxton (prefixes)

"Way Back into Love" – Hugh Grant & Haley Bennett (present perfect)

There are various ways that to use songs in lessons. For example, students can fill in the blanks as they listen to the lyrics, or notice examples of a specific grammar point and write them down. This works quite well with finding all the examples of a certain verb tense. The examples that the students find could lead to a discussion about their own thoughts and opinions about the content of the song. Finally, students could try their hand at writing one more verse (using the target grammar of course) for the song in small groups.

Use Short Stories or Cartoons

Besides songs, another fun way to teach English grammar is through short stories or cartoons. These cover just about any topic or grammatical point that you might want.

If you're very organized, consider starting a spreadsheet labelled stories and then one for cartoons. For every one that you run across, add them to your spreadsheet and label them with topic and grammar or vocabulary points. That way, you'll have a ready resource to use in the future when lesson planning.

How do you actually use these things for teaching grammar? There are various things you can do:

- Students can read the story or cartoon while noticing examples of a specific grammar point.
- You can leave blanks in the story or cartoon and students have to fill them in with the correct grammar (subject-verb agreement for example).
- Students can make their own cartoon focused on a specific theme that lends itself to the grammar point you're teaching. For example: "My Terrible Day" if you've just covered the simple past.
- Use a short story filled with your target grammar for an activity or game. For example, you might use a running dictation activity, which I'll talk about later in the book.

Don't Forget About Context

Context is key when teaching any sort of grammar. You can teach all the grammar that you want, but if students don't know how, or when to actually use it in real life, you've mostly just wasted your time.

Setting the context happens at the start of the lesson. Get students thinking about a certain situation that happens. For example, some problems they've had in the past month (late for school, didn't pay a bill on time, etc.). Then, when teaching conditionals later on in your lesson, it'll make a lot more sense (If I'm late for school, the teacher will get mad at me. If I don't pay my bills on time, the company may cut off my service).

So, forget the random grammar teaching and go for context. Pick a theme (textbooks often do this for you) and stick with it for the entire lesson. It'll help make your English lessons that much more memorable.

Grammar Requires Other Skills to Teach It

Teaching grammar is almost impossible without incorporating other skills into your lesson (reading, listening, speaking or writing). The only way to teach grammar without students learning it through the four language skills is to lecture. Is this useful? Not at all so just avoid it!

Instead, get students talking to each other about a certain topic to set the context. Or, they could watch a quick *YouTube* video and answer some simple questions about it. Then, get into a reading or listening passage filled with examples of the grammar point. After that, students can do a writing task where they do some controlled practice in a worksheet. Finally, round out the class with some interesting activities or games. As you can see, all sorts of skills are covered here in this "grammar" lesson.

Brush up on the Grammar Yourself

I remember when I first started teaching university students. It was a real struggle because I wasn't that solid on English grammar. Sure, I could take a page or two from the textbook and prepare a reasonable lesson. But, I struggled to answer any questions that my students had or tie everything together in a comprehensive way.

What really pushed me to learn English grammar was taking the CELTA and DELTA courses. They are English teaching certifications that are among the best in the business in terms of quality and worldwide recognition. Plus, they both have considerable English grammar components.

Beyond taking a teacher training course, consider going through something like the "*English Grammar in Use*" series. You can find it easily on *Amazon*. It's for English learners, but teachers would benefit greatly from it as well if they're weak on grammar. At the very least, it'll help you learn the rules and the reason behind why things are the way they are. Or consider the book, "*How to Teach Grammar*" by Scott Thornbury. It's also available on

Amazon.

Keep It Simple

With English, there are usually the basic rules and then, depending on the grammar point, there may be a ton of exceptions. When teaching, keep it simple and hit the highlights, especially for beginners. It's easy for students to get overwhelmed with too much too fast, so resist the temptation to cover every single thing.

My general rule is that it's better for students to know a few things well, rather than lots of things that they cannot consistently and correctly use. If you agree with this principle, then keep it simple when planning your lessons! Sure, touch on a few exceptions to rules, but not at the beginning and not all at once. Why not include 1-2 examples of the most common exceptions to the rule during your controlled practice worksheet and deal with them then?

Use this English Grammar Lesson Plan Template

Let's look at a way to plan and teach a grammar lesson that is both effective and enjoyable. We'll go step-by-step through a teaching process that will really involve your students in the lesson and help them understand the rules—without long, complicated explanations.

Stage 1: The Lead-in

Instead of saying, "Today we're going to learn some grammar," start your lesson by getting students engaged in an interesting, relatable topic. Think about a situation in which the grammar you're teaching is likely to occur, and get students thinking about that—not about the grammar itself just yet.

For example, for a lesson on the causative structure (to have something done), you might consider that it would be easy to use this structure when talking about rich people or celebrities, who can afford to have a lot of things done for them. If you're using a course book, you can also just use whatever topic is presented on the page. In order to get students involved, pose a direct question. For instance, you could say, "Who is your favorite celebrity and why?" Then let the students discuss their thoughts in pairs for a few minutes.

Stage 2: Present the Grammar

The key to introducing the grammar is that it should be in context. Instead of just saying, "Now we're going to learn the causative," you want to show students examples of the causative structure that are somehow related to what they discussed in the lead-in.

After the lead-in about celebrities, you could give the students a picture of someone famous, like David Beckham, along with several sentences about him written in the causative structure (it's ok if you have to make these up!):

- David Beckham has his meals cooked for him by a special chef.

- He got his favorite suit made in Paris.

- He has his car washed every day.

In doing this, you're presenting the grammar in a way that has meaning and relevance; the students can start to understand what the structure means and why it's used, because they can relate it to a real-life topic they were just discussing.

Stage 3: "Teach" the Grammar

The goal is to for students to be able to use this grammatical structure. And in order to do that, students need to be taught the meaning, form, and pronunciation of the structure. For many teachers, this is where the lecture starts. They think it's their job to tell the students all of this information. If you're not careful, this stage can turn into a long, teacher-fronted ramble that the students struggle to follow. Looking for a better way?

Try a Guided Discovery for Teaching Grammar

A guided discovery is a worksheet or activity that helps students understand a particular grammar structure. The magic of a guided discovery is that it prompts the students to figure out the rules on their own, instead of being spoon-fed the information by the teacher. This means the students will be more engaged, more empowered, and ultimately more invested during the learning process. Here's how a guided discovery works:

Use the same context and examples from earlier in the lesson. In this lesson about the causative, for instance, you would use the photo and sentences about David Beckham. Put these at the top of your guided discovery worksheet so students have clear examples to use in their exploration of the structure.

Next, create leading questions and short exercises that help the students understand what the structure means, how it's used, and how it's formed.

Stage 4: Practice the Target English Grammar

Now the students need a chance to practice what they've learned. Here are a couple of fun, interactive practice ideas for the causative structure.

Try out this Survey Activity

Have the students write two or three questions they would like to ask all of their classmates, using the causative structure. For example:

How often do you get your hair cut? (more adverb of frequency activities here)

If you could have your living room re-painted, what color would you choose?

Would you rather have your house cleaned for you or your meals cooked for you?

Let the students choose what they want to ask. As they write their survey questions, monitor to help them and correct errors as needed. Then tell the students they need to collect data from all the other students on the questions they wrote. They should all get up and mingle, asking all of the other students in class their questions and recording the answers.

Consider a Gallery Walk

A gallery walk involves putting pictures or prompts around the room and letting students walk around discussing each one—just like in an art gallery! For this lesson on the causative, you could post pictures of famous people around the room, and let students go from picture to picture, speculating about what each celebrity has done for them.

There are plenty of other activities and games to consider for getting students to practice English grammar. Check out this book on *Amazon* for some of best ones:

39 No-Prep/Low-Prep ESL Grammar Activities for Teenager and Adults.

Tips for Teaching Reading

It's Not Just About Reading for Detail

It's easy to focus most of our reading activities on reading for detail. By that, I mean that students read a text and then answer some comprehension questions. However, there's a lot more to it and there are a huge range of reading sub-skills to consider working on. For example:

- Skimming

- Scanning

- Taking notes

- Fluency

- Predicting

- Etc.

Here's some more information about the most important ones:

Reading Fluency

When reading something in a language that's not our first one, it's easy to get bogged down trying to understand every single word. This usually comes at the expense of reading fluency.

However, fluency is important not just in speaking but in reading as well. After all, nobody wants an employee who takes two hours to understand a report in English that should have taken 20 minutes to figure out. Working on scanning and skimming (see below) can help with this.

Scanning

We often have to scan or look for specific facts in a text. There are a countless examples of this, but here just a few:

- Looking for the temperature in a recipe
- Finding out what time a specific bus or plane leaves at
- Searching for a weather report on a specific day in a specific city
- Getting a certain fact to reference for a research paper

The key thing is that this should happen very quickly and if we allow our students too much time to do these tasks, it mostly defeats the purpose of it as it becomes more about reading for detail (see below).

Skimming

Skimming is similar to scanning but the key difference is that it's reading rapidly to gain a general overview of something, instead of looking for something specific. A nice way to help our students with this is to give them some very simple true/false questions about a text and then a very, very limited amount of time for a very quick first read-through. After that, they can answer the questions and then have more time for a detailed reading.

Reading for Detail

There are many times when we have to read something thoroughly and in detail in order to understand the finer points of it. This is probably the reading sub-skill that most English teachers are very familiar with.

Predicting

Prediction is a key skill for both listening and reading. The reason for this is that if we can predict what's coming, we'll likely be able to understand it more deeply and easily. One simple way to help our students with this is to show them a headline and then have them predict some things about it. For example, what questions will be answered in the reading, some key vocabulary words they might hear, or a general overview of what the reading might be about.

Recognizing Links/Understanding Discourse Markers

All texts are organized in some fashion and have various discourse markers throughout. The purpose of a discourse marker is to organize a text into segments or sections. One simple example is in a lecture where the speaker might use, "First, second, third, finally."

In addition, most texts have links between sections and sentences to assist with understanding. One simple example is the following sentences, "JOHN came home late last night. HE . . ." Or, formal essays often have a transition sentence to link paragraphs together and they'll also have a sentence in the conclusion that restates the thesis statement from the introduction.

Inferring Meaning from Context/Guessing the Meaning of Unknown Words

When reading, there are often words that we don't know, even when reading in our first language. This is the same experience that our students have when reading something in English. However, by understanding the context, either the bigger picture of the entire text, or the smaller picture as in the surrounding words, we can often guess what the word we don't know means. This allows for far more fluent reading!

If a student asks me what a certain word means, I'll ALWAYS get them to make a guess first. They're often right!

Proofreading/Editing

Proofreading and editing are vital skills for the writing process. They are also considered to be reading sub-skills because they are essentially a very close reading of a text in order to look for errors.

Inferring Attitude/Feeling/Meaning

Most things that we read, particularly fiction or things like advice columns have attitudes, feelings or meanings behind the words. Understanding what they are can influence the reading of the text and can also assist with understanding the bigger picture.

Note Taking

Note taking is a writing sub-skill that can either be done with listening as in the case of a lecture, or through reading as in the case of a report. It's a skill that most English learners struggle with because it requires identifying only the key or main points of the text.

Reading Out Loud

Although some students may be fluent when it comes to reading inside their head, they may struggle with pronunciation and reading out loud. We can help them out with this skill by giving them some practice with it in class.

Identifying Words or Grammatical Constructions

The most basic reading sub-skill is understanding words and grammatical constructions. This is often where beginners are at as things like note-taking, inferring attitudes, or recognizing discourse markers are most certainly too complex for them in most cases.

Identifying the Text Type/Purpose/Organization

Every text is written for a reason. Identifying this reason, along with the kind of text it is and the basic organizational structure can greatly assist with understanding it.

Consider Students' Needs

In terms of needs for our students when it comes to reading, there are obviously some very different ones. Compare for example someone who wants to improve their reading skills to make reading menus in restaurants when traveling easier to someone who wants to understand complicated scientific journals. Of course, improving reading skills for English proficiency tests is another major reason why students may be in our class.

If you're not sure what kinds of needs your students have, ask them! Then, do your best to tailor your lessons to their specific situations. I generally try to focus some class time to general reading skills and then some time to the specific reading needs of the students.

Vocabulary is Important

If you've ever studied another language, maybe you've had the experience of understanding almost nothing of what you read because your vocabulary was quite limited. We've all been there and it's certainly a stressful experience.

If your students are quite weak when it comes to vocabulary, then you'll have to be especially careful at selecting reading passages. They should be challenging to our students but not so challenging that they're overwhelming. Of course, they can also be useful tools for learning new vocabulary so consider pre-teaching some words that you think your students may not be familiar with before getting started.

Finally, if your students have a very limited vocabulary range, consider incorporating some work on this in your classes. This will help students significantly in all areas on English, not just reading. Take a look at these two books on *Amazon* for some games and activities designed to help students with vocabulary acquisition:

39 ESL Vocabulary Activities for Kids

39 ESL Vocabulary Activities for Teenagers and Adults

Use a Variety of Comprehension Questions

When it comes to comprehension questions, I like to mix things up a little bit and keep my students on their toes! This means a wide variety of question styles including true/false, multiple choice, as well as open-ended ones. In general, I'll have students answer the questions on their own, then compare with a partner and finally we'll check them as a class.

However, if students are focusing on reading skills for a specific English proficiency exam, then the majority of the questions should be similar in style to that so that they can some practice with that.

Does it Apply to Real-Life?

I find that the best reading lessons are those that can apply to real life. This means choosing topics and texts carefully. Hopefully our students can learn some new things as well as improve their reading skills! Or, think to themselves, "That's how I feel a lot too!," or, "My experience is the same as that person." When students have these kinds of moments, the lesson will be far more memorable which will go a long way towards our students improving their skills.

Sneak in Some Pronunciation

During my years of teaching, I've run across some students with a very impressive vocabulary and excellent reading skills. Except when they spoke or read out loud, I discovered that they had terrible pronunciation! It always surprises me, but it's certainly a real thing that can happen with some students who mostly study on their own without a conversation partner or teacher.

It's for this reason that I like to include some pronunciation work in my lessons of the particularly difficult words. Another option is to have students read out loud, either in class or as a homework assignment (it can be recorded as a *YouTube* video or audio recording).

Tips for Choosing Topics for ESL Reading Lessons

There are a few things to keep in mind when choosing topics for a reading lesson.

Choose Timeless Topics

If I'm going to put the time and effort into planning an ESL reading lesson, then I want to be able to use it again in the future. This means that I choose timeless, evergreen topics that are of interest to a wide group of people and ages. If I do this, I'll have plenty of opportunities to recycle the lesson in the future.

The Social Sciences usually have a wealth of good stories, materials and topics that lead to a great conversation. Once you plan a few of these reading lessons, you'll have a variety of go-to lessons to use over and over again.

Use *Google Drive*

In order to recycle reading lesson plans effectively, use *Google Drive*. It's possible to go in there, make a few quick changes and have a "new" lesson ready to go in just a few minutes.

Base your Lesson Plan on an Article

Of course, a *reading lesson* should be based on an article of some kind. This is obvious, but it's worth noting. You can find them online, or in textbooks.

Don't be Afraid to Adapt the Language

If you want to talk about a certain topic, but can't find an appropriate article, don't be afraid to take one and adapt the language. I usually do the following:

- Shorten the article
- Remove complicated vocabulary and terms
- Take out complicated grammatical constructions or parts of speech

Keep the Reading Short

Unless a class is 3-4 hours long, keep the reading reasonably short. In general, it shouldn't take students more than 1/5 of the class time to read the article. Sure, it's possible to assign it for homework but many students won't complete it so I like to give class time for this.

Use Authentic Materials for Higher-Level Students

For students who are at a high-intermediate or advanced level, it can be very motivating to use authentic materials. By authentic materials, I mean things like restaurant menus, newspapers and magazines, travel brochures, etc. that are designed for English speakers and not for ESL/EFL students. These can often be far more interesting than what's in a textbook and are a nice change of pace for students.

Teach Reading Strategies

The reading strategies to teach depends heavily on the genre of writing. However, some things to consider teaching are:

− Finding the thesis statement and topic sentences

− Checking for transitional words or phrases

− Reading the first and last sentences of each paragraph first

− Circling key vocabulary words

− Taking notes in the margins about main points

− Reading the comprehension questions first whenever possible

Use this 7 Step ESL Reading Lesson Plan

There are a few distinct steps to follow when teaching reading skills. Although the reading passage changes, the steps do not! First of all, be clear about the objectives of the lesson. That is, what is the lesson trying to achieve and what will success for the students look like?

Step #1: Set the Context

Context is everything when learning a language. Without it, our students are just learning random bits of grammar and vocabulary but they don't have a way to put it together into a cohesive system within their brains.

To start the lesson off, do this 100% of the time. A great teacher never forgets this! And of course, the context for each lesson will change from day to day so don't use the same old stale thing, okay?

ALWAYS help your students by providing as much context as possible either by activating prior knowledge (works well with reading or listening lessons) or give your students situations in which they can use the language (vocabulary or grammar lessons).

An easy way to do this in a reading or listening lesson is have students talk together for a couple minutes about something. During my CELTA course, I had this story about a man who was living in an airport. I was lucky, perhaps, in that it was something that the students were really interested in! In order to set the context, I had students talk about five things that people do when they have to wait in the airport for a long time (sleep/watch TV/eat + drink, etc.).

Step #2: Pre-Reading Task

This is where you have students do something related to the reading. It's possible to teach/have students review some of the key vocabulary in the passage, or do something like a prediction task.

In the case I mentioned previously, I told my students that they were going to read a story about a guy who lived in an airport for 17 years. And that he only left eventually because he got sick and had to go to the hospital. The students had to guess why they think he stayed there so long.

I elicited five answers and wrote them on the board to lead into the step #3, making sure that one of the answers was the correct one.

Step #3: Gist Reading Task

Students should always read for gist in any reading lesson. This is because it gets them out of the extremely bad habit they often have of reading every single word in excruciating detail. When people read in their first language, they never read all the words. Instead, they just skim or scan the page to look for the information they need.

Students need practice doing this in English. It's also useful if they're doing any sort of English examinations because they often contain quite long reading passages which students have to digest in a limited amount of time. Teaching students how to read and only look for specific information can be very useful.

For the airport example, I gave students only two minutes and they had to quickly skim through the passage to find out why the man stayed in the airport for so long. Always have students compare answers with each other and then check as a class. But, this is a gist reading task so give the correct answer but do NOT go into any sort of depth. Students will have another chance in the next task to catch all the nuances of the passage.

Step #4: Main Reading Task

This is where students take a more detailed look at the reading and can read more slowly and carefully. Consider using short answer, true/false questions, etc. However, at this stage I try to break students of another bad habit: always looking at their cell-phone dictionaries. I tell them that they can use it only one time, but otherwise they can just guess and use the surrounding context to give them some clues.

Students compare answers with a partner or small group and then check together as a class. It's possible to go into a bit more depth with explanations at this stage if necessary. Also consider working on some pronunciation at this time if there are any problem words.

Step #5: Application

In this stage, students take the ideas and go a bit deeper with them. For the airport example, I had students work together with a partner to think of five interesting questions that they'd ask the man if they had the chance to meet him in person.

After that, I had one person pretend to be a journalist while the other one had to be the man in the airport. The journalist conducted an interview and made sure to ask a few follow-up questions as well. I finished off the lesson by talking about what eventually happened to the man (I looked it up on the Internet).

Step #6: Homework (Optional)

You may wish to assign some homework to your students as a way to follow-up. Or, add some optional worksheets to your online tool for students to use if they'd like to.

Step #7: Post-Reading Activities

You may wish to include some post-reading activities into your classes. These can extend an hour long class into a two-hour one for example. Or, you may wish to do it over two classes. Some of the things you can do with your students are to have them think more deeply about the characters or plot.

Students can:

- Find examples of a certain part of speech
- Search for examples of a certain grammar point
- Look for metaphors and similes

- Do some worksheets
- Watch some videos about the same topic
- Listen to some related songs
- Something fun (get creative!)
- Do some kind of writing activity
- Etc.

Can I Adapt this ESL Lesson Plan Template for my Own Purposes?

Isn't it a good idea to make a lesson plan of my own? Maybe, but maybe not. Of course you can feel free to do whatever you want in your own classes (as long as it's okay with the school). Some things may work for you, while others may not.

That said, when just starting out, it can be valuable to stick pretty closely to the steps in this lesson plan sample. It's a proven system that many, many teachers around the world have been using for years and is taught in the CELTA/DELTA courses. It's backed by some solid education theory about learning languages.

More experienced teachers can consider adapting it to their own style, section by section. You know what works best for you, and your students. It's a big world out there and no two students are the same! The best teachers can adapt.

Before You Go

If you found these ESL teaching tips useful, please head on over to *Amazon* and leave a review. It will help other teachers like you find the book. Also be sure to check out my other books on *Amazon* at www.amazon.com/author/jackiebolen.

Made in United States
Troutdale, OR
08/17/2023